Bilingualism in the primary school

Over the past few years bilingualism has come to be seen not as a hindrance, but as an asset which, properly nurtured, will benefit children's linguistic awareness, cultural sensitivity and cognitive functioning. *Bilingualism in the Primary School* gives primary teachers a window on the experience of the bilingual children in their care. It helps them to make the most of what the children and their parents have to offer, giving those children a good start in the National Curriculum.

The book covers three main areas: first, the ways in which bilingual children in school can learn English and at the same time have their first languages incorporated naturally into the curriculum; second, various approaches to the assessment of oral language (including children's mother tongue); and, finally, the bilingual experience of children, teachers and parents within the wider community. Many of the contributors to the book are themselves bilingual and are thus able to understand the children's experience from within, but they are also particularly careful to show monolingual teachers how to make use of children's mother tongue experience. The book is based throughout on rich case study material of individual children at various stages on the bilingual spectrum.

Richard Mills has taught in England, Australia and Pakistan, the last with Punjabi, Urdu and Pashtu speakers, and is now Principal Lecturer and In-Service Co-ordinator at Westhill College, Birmingham. He is the author of numerous books, including *Observing Children in the Primary Classroom* (Routledge, 1988).

Jean Mills has taught in Canada and Australia, and has over fourteen years teaching experience in UK inner-city schools, mostly as a language support teacher. She has also been Deputy of the Primary ESL Unit in Birmingham LEA and is currently Senior Lecturer at Westhill College, Birmingham. Her publications include co-authorship of the *Choices* series (Oxford University Press).

Bilingualism in the primary school

A handbook for teachers

Richard W. Mills and Jean Mills

London and New York

First published 1993
by Routledge
11 New Fetter Lane, London EC4P 4EE

Simultaneously published in the USA and Canada
by Routledge

© 1993 Richard W. Mills and Jean Mills

Typeset in Palatino by Michael Mepham, Frome, Somerset
Printed and bound in Great Britain by
Biddles Ltd, Guildford and King's Lynn

British Library Cataloguing in Publication Data
A catalogue record for this book is available from the British
Library.

Library of Congress Cataloging-in-Publication Data
has been applied for.
   ISBN 0–415–08860–7
         0–415–08861–5 (pbk)

Contents

Figures and tables

FIGURES

TABLES

Contributors

Sandra Hamilton has some twenty years' experience of teaching in inner-city primary schools, including a period of home–school liaison work. Latterly she has been engaged in teacher training and is currently a lecturer in education at Loughborough University.

Sukhwant Kaur has experience of nursery and infant school teaching at a large primary school. She is currently a member of the Language Support Service on Humberside. She is bilingual in English and Punjabi.

Nabela Amin Mann teaches in a medium-sized, culturally diverse primary school in the West Midlands, where she currently has responsibility for a class of Year Two children, aged 6–7. She is multilingual in English, Punjabi and Urdu.

Jean Mills has taught since the 1970s in nursery, infant and junior schools in England, and lectured in higher education in Canada and Australia. Author of several books and articles on education, she was formerly Acting Deputy of the Language Support Service in a large West Midlands Local Authority. She is now Senior Lecturer in Education at Westhill College of Higher Education, in Birmingham.

Richard Mills taught for ten years in English schools before moving into teacher education. Having lectured in Pakistan and Australia, he is currently Principal Lecturer and In-Service Co-ordinator at Westhill College of Higher Education, in Birmingham. He is the author/editor of some twenty books on education.

Bimla Sidhu teaches in a primary school of some 280 children in the East Midlands, where she is responsible for a class of Year One children, aged 6–7. She is multilingual in English, Hindi, Punjabi and Urdu.

Acknowledgements

We are glad to acknowledge the generous help given by headteachers and staff who allowed our research to be conducted in their schools and classrooms and, of course, by the children, parents and teachers who are the subjects of the pages which follow. We readily acknowledge our debt to them, as to certain of our colleagues at Westhill College and in the Birmingham LEA Primary ESL Unit, from whom we have been glad to learn.

Chapter 3 is based on articles which appeared in *Language Observed* and *Time to Assess*, published in 1991 by the National Primary Centre.

The charts on pp. 74–8 are used with kind permission of Joan Tough.

We wish to record our particular thanks to our contributor colleagues for their efficient and committed participation, to Gill Rose for her constant interest and encouragement, and to Mari Shullaw, Routledge editor, for responding so positively (and quickly) to our letters.

Finally, as joint editors we wish to thank each other. Readers might think this an odd acknowledgement, but we have now collaborated on so many books that we sometimes find it difficult to remember who wrote what, so numerous have been the drafts. And never a cross word. Well, hardly ever.

The book is dedicated to our two sons, Robin and Peter, whose language we enjoy listening to, and who have taught us, if not all we know, then quite a lot.

R.W.M. and J.M.

Setting the scene

Richard Mills

> I speak English because I learned Polish at the age of two. I have forgotten every word of Polish, but I learned language. Here, as in other human gifts, the brain is wired to learn.
>
> (Jacob Bronowski 1973)

Many schools in large urban areas of Britain have a number of bilingual pupils. These schools may fall into one of two categories:

(a) Those that have substantial numbers of children who speak a South Asian language (Bengali, Gujerati, Punjabi, Urdu), and smaller groups, or individual children, who speak languages such as Arabic, Cantonese, Pushtu. (For instance, 8-year-old Kim was the only Vietnamese-speaking child in her school of four hundred boys and girls who spoke seven languages between them.)
(b) Those that do not have substantial numbers of bilingual children, but rather, small groups, or individuals, who speak one of the languages mentioned above, or a language from elsewhere in the world (e.g. Korean, Portuguese, Spanish, Turkish).

Developing bilingual children come as new arrivals in school from different backgrounds. They may be:

- joining the rest of the family who are already settled in Britain;
- accompanying parents who have come to study or work for a few years;
- arriving as refugees from a civil disturbance;
- attending a new school as British-born children who speak varying amounts of English at home.

These are children of the 1990s. Had they been of the 1960s the attitude towards their languages would have been very different.

At that time, teachers acknowledged the 'difference, if not the diversity' (Taylor and Hegarty 1985), in the religion, culture and language of the newcomers, as opposed to the so-called 'host community'. The terms used then and now are crucial to an understanding of the ways in which attitudes have changed. 'Difference' implies departure from a norm; 'diversity' signifies varied richness. 'Host' implies that those to be greeted are (temporary?) guests.

The whole 'multicultural' debate is, in fact, full of language time bombs. For instance, the term 'immigrants' has now acquired such pejorative overtones that it can hardly be used in school without giving offence. In its place is something like the phrase, 'members of ethnic minority communities'. One suspects it is only a matter of time before the inadequacy of those words is recognized.

The problem is that we use shorthand terms to explain complex phenomena. This is nowhere more clearly evident than in our use of the terms 'mother tongue' and 'bilingual'. 'Mother tongue' is variously used to describe:

- the first language a child speaks;
- the language invariably used at home (the 'home language');
- the language in which the user is most competent;
- the language of the community.

None of these is adequate. A speaker may have lost the use of first language; more than one language may be used at home; competence may depend on context and audience.

A better term, perhaps, is 'preferred language',

> as a substitute for the notions of dominant language, mother tongue or L1, since it brings out clearly the varying nature of bilingual proficiency.

> (Baetens Beardsmore, 1986)

This term was coined by Dodson (1981) and is attractive since it takes some account of personal choice and possible changes across time and context. Perhaps, also, the concept has about it a certain status and, as such, may be helpful in combating what Skutnabb-Kangas (1990) refers to as 'linguicism', i.e. language prejudice, akin to racism and sexism.

Such language prejudice was seen vividly back in the 1960s assimilationist phase when teachers, schools and Local Education Authorities were strongly urging that incoming children use English only. Popular report has it that children were spoken of as 'having no language', meaning no English language, and were exhorted to 'speak only English'. The concept of 'verbal deficit' was common, alongside the notion of 'first language interference'. As Chatwin (1984) suggests:

Since languages other than English would be thought to obstruct or delay pupils' acquisition of English, their use would be discouraged. All non-standard usages would be corrected.

Such a view of English language insularity is akin to the notion of racial purity; mixing implies contamination. In fact, any language in a dynamic society is itself dynamic; it is constantly evolving in response to the demands of time, attitudes, context. To speak of 'first language interference' is to present that first language negatively, not as something to build on but, rather, as an unwelcome hindrance.

A much richer, all-embracing notion is that of 'interlanguage' (Selinker, 1972), used to refer to an individual learner's own language system. Here there is movement back and forth between two or more languages, as the learner makes use of existing knowledge to forge new understanding. The stress is on process, rather than product, and acceptability of 'errors' is as justifiable in this area as it is in any other realm of developing understanding, whether it be mathematics or morality, science or psychology. The so-called 'errors' are a genuine part of the learning; indeed, without them there would be no learning to take place. They are a sign that learning can occur. As Cook (1991) writes of interlanguage:

> Learners are not wilfully distorting the native system; they are inventing a system of their own. No-one is claiming that the learner's interlanguage takes precedence over the version of the native speaker. That, after all, is where the learners are, in a sense, heading.

Many instances quoted in the chapters which follow represent the full spectrum of language use, from interdependence to interchangeability, from interlanguage to code-switching, where speakers who are bilingually proficient move imperceptibly between languages.

What is more, they are now encouraged to do so in many schools, so great has been the change in the last thirty years. In the memorable (albeit sexist, expression) of the Bullock Report (1975):

> No child should be expected to cast off the language and culture of the home as he crosses the school threshold, nor to live and act as though school and home represent two totally separate and different cultures which have to be kept firmly apart. The curriculum should reflect many elements of that part of his life, which a child lives outside school.

This is in line with Plowden, of course, and the crucial educational concept of moving from the known to the unknown. Bullock, however, goes further in seeing bilingualism in itself as something to be cared for and sustained:

Their bilingualism is of great importance to the children and their families, and also to society as a whole. In a linguistically conscious nation in the modern world, we should see it as an asset, as something to be nurtured, and one of the agencies which should nurture it is the school.

The term 'bilingualism' is here used by Bullock in an apparently undifferentiated sense. In fact, the word is capable of many subtleties of definition, which include such modifiers as: Achieved, Additive, Ascendant, Ascribed, Asymmetrical, Balanced, Compound, Consecutive, Co-ordinate, Covert, Diagonal, Dormant, Functional, Horizontal, Incipient, Passive, Productive, Receptive, Recessive, Residual, Secondary, Simultaneous, Societal, Subordinate, Subtractive, Successive, Vertical.

I mention these not merely to indicate an acquaintance with the index of Baetens Beardsmore (1986), but to alert readers to the fact that, whenever the terms 'bilingual' and 'bilingualism' are used in the pages which follow, the precise definition cannot constantly be supplied. To do so would be both tedious and counter-productive. Instead, the terms are best understood if the modifier 'developing' (perversely, not used by Baetens Beardsmore) is taken as read. In other words, children whom we describe as 'bilingual' are, in fact, 'developing bilinguals'. Each is somewhere along the spectrum which has 'monolingual' at one end and 'balanced bilingual' or 'code-switcher' at the other.

Furthermore, there is the question of the place of language within the multicultural debate. If we grant that the current position in our thinking is one of 'cultural pluralism', then the stance we take in this book towards bilingualism or multilingualism can be seen to be consistent. I use the term 'cultural pluralism' to reflect the accepted co-existence of two or more mutually respected and respectable ways of behaving and living. Language, as a sub-set of behaviour, comes within this definition.

This being so, a balance needs to be vigilantly maintained by, and on behalf of, developing bilingual children. As the NCMTT (1985) has it:

> To learn English to the highest level possible is important, but so is the fostering and nurturing of one's first language. One without the other cannot be called 'pluralism'.

Such a balance appears to have eluded the National Curriculum English Working Group in their statement (1988):

> The key to equality of opportunity, to academic success and, more broadly, to participation on equal terms as a full member of society, is good command of English, and the emphasis must, therefore, we feel, be on the learning of English.

One wonders what concept of 'society' the authors had in mind when they wrote these words and it is interesting to balance this statement against another National Curriculum document, that for Modern Foreign Languages (1990):

> There should be no restrictions on bilingual pupils studying the language of their home or community as their first foreign language.

Our stance in this book is that the learning of English is vital. But then so, also, is the maintenance and development of one's mother tongue. If the balance is right, the expectation is that each will feed off and enhance the other, to the benefit of the learner, in terms of language, cultural sensitivity and cognitive functioning. (See Baker, 1988: Chapter 2, for a discussion of these potential benefits.)

Most of our case studies and examples are of children who speak Punjabi (often spelled 'Panjabi'). This language is spoken in the Punjab, the historic region now divided between India and Pakistan. Indian Punjabi speakers are mainly Sikh or Hindu and in Britain originate largely from the Punjab, neighbouring states or East Africa. While Sikh Punjabi speakers use the Gurmukhi script for literacy, many Hindu Punjabi speakers will read and write in Hindi. Pakistani Punjabi speakers in Britain are mainly Muslim and use Urdu for literacy and religious instruction. Many come from the Mirpur region of Pakistan and speak Mirpuri Punjabi.

This, then, is the background of most of the children we focus on in this book. Different linguistic points could be made about children whose first language is, say, Arabic, Bengali, Cantonese or Greek, but we believe that the major premises we advance, in terms of culture maintenance, assessment in mother tongue, bilingual benefits, community involvement, and so forth, remain fairly constant, and would apply to most non-English language groupings in school. Our guiding principle throughout is that concentrating upon individual children is not only valid in itself but, ultimately, more productive in revealing processes and forces at work within the larger communities.

The book is divided into three sections. We begin with the school as a language community and the individual child within that community. We move on to consider the specific issue of language assessment, and we end with a focus on the bilingual experience itself and a looking forward to the involvement of the wider community in bilingual education.

All the members of our team of contributors are bilingual in some sense (although, to some of us, the term does not come naturally). As with children in school, so we have tried to learn from each other, as we hope the contents and authorship will indicate.

Finally, as a demonstration of changing attitudes to language acquisition, it is worth recalling that Tacitus records the legend of how, after the defeat of a Roman army in Germany in AD 9, the Germans cut out the tongues of Roman prisoners and ate them, in the belief that they would thereby learn Latin. We are not, in this book, recommending such an approach. We do not know if it worked.

Note: Italics are used throughout the book where quoted extracts were spoken in the mother tongue and have been reported in English for clarity.

Section I

Living and learning in two languages

Chapter 1

Language activities in a multilingual school
Jean Mills

EDITORS' INTRODUCTION

Many primary schools undertake language awareness and language study courses, in line with National Curriculum requirements. Multilingual schools are ideally placed for this work in that their resources, in terms of children, staff, other professionals, and parents, are often substantial and always to hand. An initial survey of Who-speaks-what-in-which-context? (see Appendix 2) will indicate some of the language riches to be mined. (A school secretary knows some Welsh songs; a child speaks four languages and is literate in two of them; a teacher learnt some Polish phrases from her parents; a dinner assistant has a strong Scots accent and dialect.)

Accordingly, this chapter describes such a survey. It also highlights several other language activities across the infant–junior range, in a school readily alert to the possibilities:

- capitalizing on story with 6-year-olds;
- using a language notice board with older infants;
- organizing a staff–children language teach-in;
- improvising with shadow puppets;
- shopping and photographing in the local High Street.

All these activities are presented with commentary and analysis. The whole aim is to show a living community drawing on its own resources for its own benefit, a vast kind of DIY exercise. Many practical ideas for language work are suggested, which are as appropriate in monolingual as in multilingual contexts.

Throughout the chapter there is a strong stress on the children's own culture and background, both as a means of confirming their identity and as a way of disseminating that experience to others. This is to take seriously Noam Chomsky's vivid aphorism, 'Language is a window on the mind' (Wells 1987) and to respond to Michael Halliday's injunction that we must 'Learn to listen to language' (1968). Our own and other people's.

A thought which does not result in an action is nothing much, and an action which does not proceed from a thought is nothing at all.

(Georges Bernanos)

The setting is a West Midlands primary school, with 230 children on roll. Over 70 per cent of the children are exposed at home to the variety of Punjabi spoken by Sikhs (a phrase chosen because of the range of competence of children and parents in this language), but there are also varying numbers of children who speak Mirpuri (a Pakistani variety of Punjabi), Bengali, Urdu and Gujerati. One family, whose origins are in the North West Frontier Province of Pakistan, speaks Pushtu; two families are from Uganda and Nigeria respectively; some children hear and speak Creole at home (indeed, two boys arrived recently from Jamaica and, at first, found communication with their peers difficult). There are also, among the children, monolingual English speakers. Apart from the classroom assistant, who is fluent in English, Urdu (both written and spoken) and Mirpuri/Punjabi, the staff would, by and large, designate themselves as monolingual English speakers. (More of this later.)

Given, then, that the school readily describes its curriculum as 'child-centred', how does it respond to such linguistic diversity?

There follows now a description of some language curriculum responses that were made in one school year by different members of staff. Responses in other areas of the curriculum and with the local community did, of course, occur, but they are not the subject of this chapter. The attempt here is to bring together some of the different threads of positive acknowledgement that 'child-centred' means, among other things, accepting children's background, culture and language, as crucial foundations on which to build. The stress, then, is not on the so-called 'problems' of linguistic diversity, but on its premises, promise and potential.

However, before the description begins, let me state my own starting-point. For the past few years my work has been as a teacher of English as a Second Language. A better term now in vogue is 'Language Support teacher'. This has nuances which more accurately reflect the way in which I and my colleagues in the English as a Second Language Department like to work. More often than not we prefer to remain in the classroom in partnership with the class teacher. When the class teacher and the Language Support teacher operate apart, neither knows the work of the other sufficiently to be able to build on it; we lose collaborative opportunities. Moreover, the term 'Support' implies recognition of the status and value of the original language(s). Important as it is for the children to learn English, this is not to be a take-over in which the original identity is submerged.

With regard to methodology, the intention is to aim for communicative performance, with the emphasis on using language in realistic situations, not practising how to use it in a classroom cocoon, as Brumfit points out (1979). The activities I am going to describe are based on the following premises:

- they have a real purpose and try to avoid atomized and isolated language exercises and drills;
- the content and purpose of language may be stressed more than practice of grammatical structures;
- authentic materials and situations will be used;
- the status of the original language(s) should be maintained, alongside the acquisition of English.

At the same time, and this will be highlighted as the chapter continues, drawing upon other languages within the school curriculum brings further benefits:

- teachers' understanding and empathy with individual children increases;
- working in several languages aids cognitive development.

A range of activities was undertaken by a variety of age groups, covering many of the National Curriculum English Attainment Targets in terms of speaking and listening, reading, writing. I am only able to describe here in detail those which involved me directly; others, which are more sketchily described, did not.

1 STORY-BASED WORK WITH MIDDLE INFANTS

The teacher of this group was keen to use simple stories as a basis for developing literacy skills in her class of 6-year-olds. We consulted and chose two stories, one for each half of the term. Both stories, 'The Six Blind Men' and 'The Foolish Tortoise', had featured on the BBC TV series *Talkabout* of which we had a video and a teachers' pack to accompany the series, containing:

six sets of pictures;
six copies of captions;
one copy of a simplified text;
one copy of a full text.

These materials constituted a foundation for the work we wanted to do.

Thus, all the children saw the video of each story and, during the viewing, we were able to pause; re-run; make particular points; check comprehension; ask a variety of evaluative, speculative and predictive questions. Some of the more confident children then retold parts of the story in their mother tongues, to the delight of the others. The children also carried out some simple role plays in small groups, supervised by the class teacher and myself.

I was particularly impressed that, once their roles were assigned, such young children could carry a story through with little or no intervention from a teacher. I suspect the fact that they had, by then, heard a story several times, with its repeated formulae, was crucial. For example, the six blind men, when feeling the elephant, say, in turn: 'It's like a ... wall ... spear ... snake ... tree-trunk ... flag ... rope.' Such a formula, once learnt, can be extended to other objects and compared by the children with the structure in their home language. Unlike monolingual children, they are thus working in two symbolic systems at an early age. This is a situation which, according to Vygotsky (1984) and others, enhances, rather than retards, cognitive development. After these preliminary activities, the children moved on to literacy skills. We were particularly fortunate that, owing to a quirk in the time-table, we had the help in one of our sessions of our newly arrived Punjabi/Urdu-speaking classroom assistant. In addition, the head teacher had gained the assistance of a volunteer communicator who spoke Bengali. (There were five Bengali-speaking children in the class, two of whom were fairly new arrivals.)

Thus, the activities could be carried out in English and three other languages. Using the story pack, the teacher had prepared:

• a cloze passage in English;
• a word search grid;
• some true/false sentences for matching.

We were also able to use the pictures and captions for:

• re-telling the story;
• sequencing (what happened next? ... before? ... after?);
• matching;
• writing original sentences.

The children sampled several of these activities in the time available. Those who spoke Bengali or Punjabi or Urdu heard the story again in their mother tongue and were supported in that language while carrying out different tasks, as well as working in English, where they would use comparable vocabulary and structures. At one point, the word processor was available and the Bengali-speaking children tried writing their sentences on it in English, helped by the Bengali communicator.

Meanwhile, in the case of the first story ('The Six Blind Men'), I was supervising children in the making of clay elephants. What language resulted from this situation?

Firstly, there was, of course, the language of social interaction: discussing the materials; making our preparations; talking about incidents in our lives, while we were working. However, alongside such social language there was, inevitably, a more pedagogic language. To this end, I focused on:

- the names for the materials and tools we were using;
- the techniques we were employing (viz. smoothing, sticking, pressing, rolling, cutting etc.);
- the sequence of activities (e.g. 'First we're going to ... now we ... then we ... after that we ...');
- the parts of the elephant's body;
- the different shapes of those parts (e.g. long, thin, pointed, fat, sharp, round etc.);
- the reasons for carrying out certain procedures ('If we don't ... then we ...');
- the eliciting of opinions ('Do you want it to ...? Do you like the way it ...?').

Almost incidental to this, and quite naturally, we began to discuss Punjabi equivalents for some of the English words and phrases we were using. For example, 'I made an elephant' was rendered (in my phonetic transliteration in Roman script) 'Me hotee benai'. Coupled with their use of mother tongue for other work they were doing, and allied to their own teacher's very obvious interest in their home languages, the children became noticeably more interested and forthcoming. They became more relaxed about using their mother tongue in school; they competed in telling a teacher things they could say; they offered to teach their teacher new words; they used the correct name for their languages (as opposed to just 'Indian' or 'Pakistani').

When the clay models were finished and children had begun painting them to look like Indian decorated elephants, I took a specific group, who needed some help with their English language development, to make a book about the process.

After much discussion, we broke it down into stages and, using cut-out shapes on each page, showed how the elephants had been put together. A simple sentence accompanied each illustration. Thus:

1 We made elephants with clay.
2 We had a lump of clay, some water, a knife and some tools.
3 First we made the body.
4 Then we made four legs.
5 Then we made the head.
6 Then we made the trunk.
7 Then we made two tusks.
8 Then we made two ears.
9 Last of all, we made the tail.
10 Baljinder says, 'I had to paint my elephant with a very little brush.'
11 Ravinder says, 'I painted my elephant with the brush. You must hold them carefully or they will break. You have to put them on the shelf.'

The next stage was to translate the book into Punjabi. Again, I copied this down using Roman script to approximate to Punjabi phonemes, for my own immediate convenience. Obviously, the next stage is for me to learn Punjabi (Gurmukhi) script. Thus:

1 Assee hotee benai see narlee essee clay laiyassee.
2 Keena clay sida benaiya see narli mool laiyassee.
3 Narlee fair assee muttated benaiyassee.
4 Fair assee char loota benaiyassee.
5 Fair assee sair benaiyassee.
6 Fair assee ek nak benaiyassee.
7 Fair assee dough audia tusk benaiyassee.
8 Fair assee dough khun benaiyassee.
9 Fair assee audi poosh benaiyassee.

Under instruction from the children, I was eventually able to read this back to them with sufficiently correct pronunciation, rhythm and stress, to enable them to understand. (Later, I checked the version with our classroom assistant. There seemed to be only one error – the children had used the expression, 'two his ears'.)

The whole process was most instructive. To begin with, it revealed different aspects of the children themselves. Although all could perform quite well in English, and I had heard them speak Punjabi to peers and adults, their ability to translate varied considerably. Two appeared to have no problems, transferring between the two languages with ease;

debating between themselves over improved versions; disagreeing about particular words. Two other children appeared either uninterested or lost by the process; they offered no contributions. Nor did this non-participation seem to depend on personality or lack of English/Punjabi, since one of the children is very outgoing, interacts well in English and speaks mainly Punjabi at home. However, as a monolingual teacher, I cannot, unaided, judge his fluency in Punjabi. On the other hand, this boy does have difficulties with maths, reading and writing, and it occurred to me later that his translation difficulty may have stemmed from dealing with abstract conceptual systems. What we needed to investigate was the stage (in Piagetian terms) which his cognitive development had reached and the level of his Punjabi.

Another aspect was equally intriguing. The children did not translate word for word, but in whole sentences. If they disagreed on a version they repeated the whole phrase rather than saying, 'It should be such and such a word'. This points to the fact that, although these young children can operate in equivalents between languages, noting changes of vocabulary, tense and so forth, they do not analyse what they are doing. Indeed, one would hardly expect them to do so, but they are clearly engaged in an intriguing process which would pay dividends in research terms.

However, what of the adult on the scene, namely, myself? Was there any value to be gained in my own observations on how I learnt? I did try to analyse what had happened and, as I reflected on the tutoring by the children, it seemed that several strategies had been applied. I had been obliged to listen for the tune of the language in order to establish appropriate pronunciation, rhythm and stress. Unlike young children I had been able to write down sentences, thereby avoiding reliance on memory. This aided memorization and made separate words and structural patterns more explicit; I was able to impose an order on what I was trying to understand. (McDonough, 1981, usefully highlights this and other strategies.) Furthermore, I was able to use previous knowledge (i.e. Latin) as a reminder of varying word order; mediators (as in 'nak' ... 'copper's nark' ... 'nose'); and syntactic strategies (i.e. looking first for function words such as adverbs and verbs). Finally, the refuge of the unconfident or the desperate, I checked with an authority (viz. the classroom assistant).

Clearly, children do not have recourse to the same kind of strategies and one must look for equivalents or alternatives they do have. They may well possess that 'single, most important factor in language learning' (Savignon in Krashen, 1981), which is attitude (including its sub-set, motivation). In this instance, they also demonstrated 'constant effort and constant involvement' (Naiman *et al.*, 1975) in a truly communicative situation. There was a genuine information gap which needed to be bridged.

The foregoing were not, however, the only ways in which these children were able to use their mother tongues in school. Their teacher also conducted the morning 'news' time in mother tongue and English, with more fluent children often translating for those who would not have expressed themselves so fully in English alone. Similarly, parts of the class assembly were translated into Punjabi. Again, the children made finger puppets which told stories in two languages. A fascinating insight emerged here when the teacher told me that some children adopted different personalities for the different languages – being serious and reserved in English but verbose, excitable and humorous in Punjabi.

As in the book-making episode, observation of children operating in two languages can be a revealing procedure and, I believe, should be a routine element in language assessment.

2 LANGUAGE AWARENESS: TOP INFANTS AND FIRST-YEAR JUNIORS

A colleague and I planned a language awareness course to last for six weeks, with me working in the classroom on a collaborative basis for two afternoons per week. The basic structure was: Communication, related to oneself; one's home; the community.

In this particular class we had a wide range of home languages to draw on: Bengali, Creole, English, Gujerati, Ika (Nigeria), Lwo (Uganda), Punjabi, Urdu. Here is a diary description of what occurred over the six weeks.

Week One

The children looked closely at their own faces and at photographs of faces depicting a range of cultures, ages and emotions. They discussed what faces could tell them. Using a mirror, they painted their own faces as accurately as possible and provided a caption to introduce themselves. This was written in English and appropriate script as a large speech bubble coming out of the mouth. This portrait gallery was displayed around the classroom walls.

Week Two

The children discussed and answered a language questionnaire detailing languages they knew about (see Appendix 2); who they spoke to in which

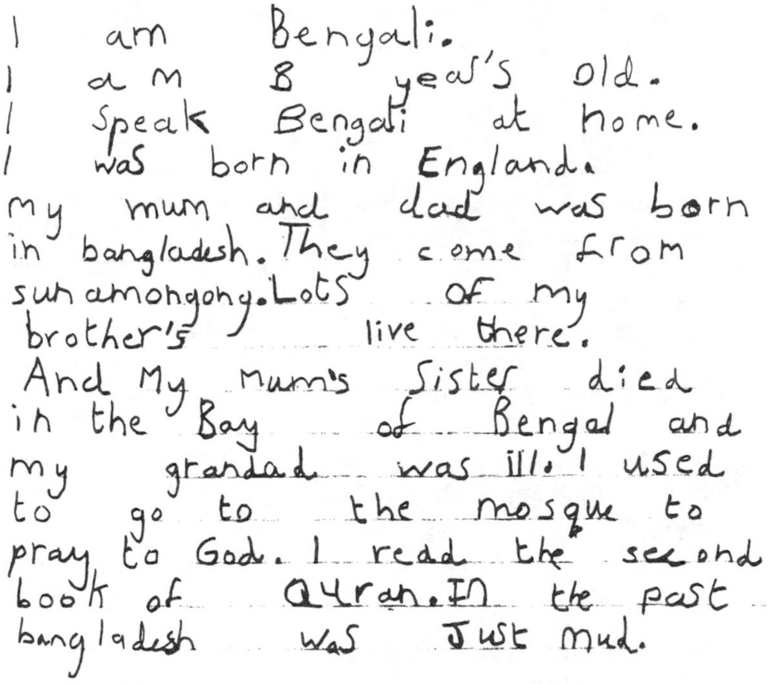

I am Bengali.
I a m 8 year's old.
I Speak Bengali at home.
I was born in England.
my mum and dad was born
in bangladesh. They come from
sun amongong. Lots of my
brother's live there.
And My mum's Sister died
in the Bay of Bengal and
my grandad was ill. I used
to go to the mosque to
pray to God. I read the second
book of Quran. In the past
bangladesh was Just mud.

Figure 1   Yeasin's piece

language; which they thought/dreamt in. Using the questionnaire as support, they all wrote about themselves. Figure 1 is Yeasin's piece.

Week Three

We discussed our names and why we had been given them. We described culturally different naming ceremonies. We made a collection in different languages of the terms for different family relationships. The children used these lists and their questionnaires to draw a map of the relationships and language of communication in their own families.

Week Four

The children had been bringing in items and extracts in different languages for display on a 'Language Board'. We looked closely at these items – newspapers, posters, calendars, letters, stamps, coins, comics, books, advertisements, bags. We compared the different scripts and made attempts at translations. The children then designed their own stamps for a country and in a language of their own choice.

Week Five

We visited the main shopping centre, taking with us a video camera and a 35 mm camera to capture on film some of the shop window fronts and advertisement posters. In the event, we recorded material from a dentist's surgery; a bookshop; a video shop; the law centre; a printer's window; posters for Bhangra groups; an election poster – all in a variety of scripts. After viewing and discussing the video, back in school later, we ate some Indian sweets which we had bought on our trip – one way to make any activity popular, if that were needed. Later that week, three mothers visited the class and talked about their lives and their children's lives in India, Nigeria and Uganda. They counted for the children in Iko, Lwo and Punjabi. One of the mothers wrote a number strip for the children in English and Punjabi.

Week Six

Language teach-in. We divided the children into small groups of three or four and sent them to different members of staff to be taught some of another language or dialect for twenty minutes. The staff had been talked into this during informal discussion when we became aware, as any staff would do, of the language riches at our disposal. We began by thinking we had little to offer. In the event, we arranged the following sessions:

- song in Glaswegian dialect (with the headteacher);
- Welsh phrases and a song (with the secretary);
- Polish greetings and counting (with a teacher whose parents were Polish);
- Bengali greetings (with the volunteer communicator);
- French greetings and counting (with an ex-secondary teacher of French);
- German greetings and counting (with a teacher who had done some German at school);
- Urdu phrases (with the classroom assistant);
- classroom commands in Bengali (taught me by two children).

As the groups returned to the classroom they were videoed, performing what they had learnt (although the secretary enjoyed it all so much that she kept her group all afternoon). A quavering rendition of 'Twa Crows' was something not to be missed. As a finale, the class was able to display what they had learnt during an assembly.

Evaluation

What was gained during those six weeks?

Firstly, the children used a wide range of language skills. Not only by working at the four cornerstones of communication (listening, speaking, reading, writing), but also by employing different functions, modes, registers, genres, within those areas. They were able to explore some of their own personal experiences and to analyse some of their own uses of language; their family situation; their community.

Above all, they were introduced, as Houlton indicates (1985), to the diverse, yet comparable, linguistic experience of others, becoming aware, in the process, that the class contained some monolingual English speakers. Thus, the premise was established that, however various our language experiences might be, we all had English in common. Unity in diversity. By the end of the project the children displayed a greater assurance about their home languages, were more at ease in discussing them, and, in the case of one child, actually admitted something she had at first denied, namely, that she could speak Punjabi.

If we had needed a maxim for our six-week project, I think it could have been, 'Make the best use you can of the resources available' (Fillmore in Krashen, 1981). Our best resource was the children themselves, however rudimentary their language knowledge (and a danger to be resisted was exaggerating their command of languages other than English, merely because one did not know those languages oneself). In addition, we had parents to call on and the immediate environment as stimulus.

However, just as interesting was the fact that, with a relatively small staff who, on the whole, would deny any special linguistic abilities, we could, nevertheless, call on so many languages and language varieties. Indeed, on reflection, there were other people we could have used as well, such as:

- a teacher who had an Austrian father;
- a teacher who had lived in Italy;
- a caretaker from the West Indies;
- several with various brands of Yorkshire, Black Country and Brummie dialects and accents.

I am sure investigation of any school staff anywhere in the country would reveal rich language resources.

3 BILINGUAL SESSIONS WITH BEGINNERS – JUNIORS

A small group of children had been in the school only a matter of months. They included three from Bangladesh (aged 11, 9, 8; the elder two being sisters); another girl (11), an Urdu speaker from Kashmir. Another Bangladeshi boy (9) had been in England almost a year but needed much oral help. Since these children came from three different classes, I departed from my normal custom and withdrew them for different sessions.

For one of these sessions I was joined by Sofia, the Bengali-speaking communicator. Together we provided opportunities for the children to explore their experiences in Bangladesh and Pakistan. Not only was it an opportunity for them to build on what they knew; it was also a chance for me to learn something of their former way of life. (I had visited Pakistan but not Bangladesh and, in any event, their experience of rural life would not be my experience as a tourist.) Moreover, since Urfa, the Urdu-speaking girl, wanted to accompany her Bengali-speaking friend, this provided another dimension, enabling us to compare three languages and cultures.

The search for stimulus material proved frustrating but ultimately yielded a set of twenty-four slides of Bangladesh; a Health Education Pack 'Looking after ourselves' (Oxfam), featuring a Bangladeshi village, with two wall charts and eleven pictures. The children particularly enjoyed viewing the slides through small, hand-held, projectors and this stimulated them to talk about incidents in their lives: a rickshaw ride with an aunty ... a visit to a mosque ... giant fish in ponds ... danger from snakes and floods. Much of this conversation was channelled, of course, through Sofia, who established a ready rapport. The children were able to tell simplified versions of their stories in English, while more complex detail emerged in the Bengali versions. Thus, Figure 2 shows Sujon's story, told in English and transcribed.

The pictures of village ponds (pukkur) prompted this story from Shaid, with the detail coming from Sofia's translation as I tried to clarify different points ('Why did you dig a pond?' ... 'Did your house get washed away?').

Shaid's story

My dad got a lot of other men, some of them were my uncles, to dig a big pond in my village. This was because, when a big wave came up the canal, it caused floods. The water didn't come to my house because it had big walls, but a lot of people's houses were broken down.

When the flood comes, big fish are washed into the pond. The men use cudahl (adze) to dig the pond. The cudahl break the stones very

One day I saw a man getting rice
then I saw a snake on the tree. Then the
man looked back then he ran. Then I ran.
I was scared it might follow me. That's what the
snakes do in Bangladesh. I think it was a
tree snake.

Sujon

Figure 2 Sujon's story

quickly. There is a pump to put water on the fields. The water is salty.
You can't drink it, but it doesn't hurt the vegetables.

There is also a well near my aunty's house. I don't go. I'm too little.
A man gets the water for us. It is his job to get the water. People pay
him to get it. He has a boat to get it. He goes on the canal. Sometimes
he takes two hours. Sometimes three hours.

Another set of pictures which interested the children showed the village
crops. Many of these seemed to be fruits, some of which were new to me.
Several of them had grown in the children's gardens or near their villages.
I decided to use this interest and knowledge as a kind of bridge between
past and present experience. The children drew as many fruits as they
could remember and we named them in English and Bengali, with Sofia
providing the Bengali script. Apart from any other advantage, this helped
me to learn more Bengali words myself and to have a further point of
contact.

The children were able to describe many of the fruits and their trees,
with little recourse to Bengali, although Sofia confirmed details. We then
visited local shops and the children chose the fruit or vegetable they
wanted me to photograph. These turned out to be: oranges, coconuts,
mangoes, pumpkins, chilli, cauliflowers, white radishes, kerela (bitter
gourd), okra. Later, back in class, the photographs provided a further
stimulus as children chose one to write about.

This, in itself, generated discussion in the form of disagreement over
how items were cooked and eaten. As I wrote down the descriptions so
the children moved naturally back and forth between Bengali and English,
with the final version being read out for agreement. The situation provided a natural way to practise tenses (past and present simple); language
for sequences; and extended vocabulary, as the two extracts (Figures 3 and
4) indicate.

By this time the festival of Eid Ul Fitr had arrived and when I mentioned
that we might make fruit chaat (like fruit salad), Urfa insisted she would
bring the ingredients for vegetable chaat also. The choosing, buying and
preparation of the fruit and vegetables became another language experience for the children and one which they were able, again, to discuss later
via a photographic record.

4 SHADOW PUPPETS: SECOND-YEAR JUNIORS

A group came into school to perform a shadow puppet play for all the
children. Later the leader of the group (a teacher herself), returned to work
collaboratively in a class of 9-year-olds, to develop a puppet play with

Urfa chose this picture.

The word for mango in Urdu is am.

It is the same in Bengali.
The green ones are sour.
When a strong wind comes it makes
the tree shake.
The mangoes fall down.

Figure 3 Extract from work produced in a bilingual lesson

Sayeda chose this picture.
She says "I have a lemon tree
in my garden in Bangladesh."
They are not big trees you can
pick the lemons very easily."

আমীনা এই ছবি পছন্দ করেছে।
সে বলেছে "আমাদের আছে। এই গাছ বড় হয় না, তুমি সহজেই লেবু তুলতে পারবে।

Figure 4 Extract from work produced in a bilingual lesson

them. This part of the description will be more distanced than others since, although I saw the end product, I was not directly involved in the build-up.

The story chosen as a basis for the play was 'The Sleeping Prince', a Spanish folktale from *Clever Gretchen and Other Forgotten Folktales* (Alison Lurie, Heinemann, 1980). The plot outline is as follows:

One winter day a princess hears a bird singing about a sleeping prince who can only be woken by a maiden who will watch over him. The princess decides to rescue the prince. She has a pair of iron shoes made and sets off on her quest. She calls at three lonely cottages and at each one has to hide from the West Wind, the East Wind and the North Wind. At each cottage she learns more about how to overcome obstacles in her path. Finally, she arrives at the castle and circumvents the dangers to find everyone asleep. She waits months until the hour of the prince's awakening comes. The grateful prince marries her and they return to her overjoyed parents. Even from this brief summary, it is possible to appreciate something of the power exerted across cultures by a good story.

This tale has several strengths:

- familiar elements (e.g. a sleeping prince);
- a potentially dangerous journey, with evil to overcome;
- the magic number three;
- repetition of formulae and verses;
- intriguing elements (such as iron shoes);
- a female protagonist, faithful, adventurous and intrepid.

Teasing out these features of world-wide stories is a legitimate part of a multicultural stance in school.

After the initial stimulus of the story itself, the class went on to carry out a variety of tasks:

- They retold the story in six sentences and pictures.
- They did some text-based work, including cloze procedure and sequencing.
- They performed pair / small group / class drama activities in English and mother tongue.
- They had a discussion on sexism and racism.
- Each child made a puppet, choosing any character they liked and experimenting with different materials to get the maximum effect from a strong light source.
- They improvised dialogue for their final performance in English and mother tongue.

- They made a screen by stretching white cloth over a large wooden frame.
- In withdrawal groups they improvised and composed music for the play.
- They learnt a Spanish song.
- In withdrawal groups they improvised the script until a final version was agreed. All children had the opportunity to record parts of the story on to tape; this ensured that everyone was included.
- Finally, the class performed their play at a special assembly for the whole school and parents.

This example, like the others, demonstrates that accepting and using the children's home languages constructively is not the procrustean process some would imagine it to be. The curriculum is neither stretched nor curtailed to include mother tongue. The process of inclusion is quite natural once the premise has been established. The result then, as I have attempted to show, puts stress on the positive benefits accruing from a multilingual classroom, rather than on its supposed 'problems' (Mercer *et al*. 1985).

AND FINALLY ...

Reports preceding the implementation of the National Curriculum (Kingman, Cox) were disturbingly thin on the multicultural classroom, but would surely have approved a situation in which exploration of language could take place as a matter of course. Indeed, the LINC (Language in the National Curriculum) initiative endorses this kind of enquiry. It may be worthwhile, then, indicating what kind of model emerges from my description of items in the school year.

Several maxims are evident:

- Language learning is an active process and best takes place in genuinely communicative situations.
- Languages are equal and have their own integrity. We should respect and value languages, dialects and accents different from our own.
- Languages are personal. They reflect individual and cultural identity. Acknowledging and attempting to learn other languages enhances individual and group esteem and gives a key to other cultures.
- Languages build bridges. The transition between home and school, and between school and community, is facilitated by multilingual communication. Recognizing children's mother tongues and incorporating them into school work increases a teacher's knowledge of the children.
- Language is thought. Learning English and learning across the curricu-

lum should be enhanced if children are bilingual. Such children are able to compare linguistic operations and the verbal expression of concepts. Bilingualism helps us to think about thinking.

- Languages need to be nurtured. What nearly happened to Welsh and Breton in the early twentieth century, and is happening to Cornish, should be a warning to us. There is a rich resource of languages, dialects, accents all around us. It does not merely reside in books; it resides in people. A child-centred approach to education starts with boys and girls, not grammar texts.

Appendix 1

Ideas for supporting English language development in mainstream classrooms

The same basic principles which underpin all good primary practice are also applicable to language teaching. That is to say, teachers should:

- begin with the needs of individual children;
- use meaningful situations that stem from normal classroom activities and are related to a child's conceptual development;
- help children to build up their own learning strategies.

Any assessment of needs will take into account such factors as: family situation; first language; previous educational experience. (For newly arrived children someone in the immediate family might be found to act as communicator.) The following links may be made:

- On occasions, someone can help in class, both to translate lesson content, and to carry out curriculum activities in the first language.
- Tapes can be passed on for parents to record dual-text stories or translations of books.
- A journal can be used for communications between teachers and parents, or so that language items can be reinforced at home.
- Someone may be able to carry on literacy work in the first language, supporting 'balanced' bilingualism.

However, if there is no-one who can help in these ways, the school needs to look further afield. Are there students in local secondary schools who speak, or are studying, particular languages, or are eager to practise their communication skills? Is there a university or college or polytechnic nearby which has bilingual students undertaking teacher training courses? Which community groups listed in the telephone book may be able to offer help or advice?

FIRST LANGUAGE

It is surprising that some schools do not see the need to discover exactly which language children speak. It is important to do so, for several reasons.

Firstly, the school may want to group children and to check on whether potential communicators are linguistically and culturally appropriate. Does the family speak a dialect or a non-standard form of the language (such as Sylheti Bengali, South American Spanish, Cantonese)?

Secondly, it is unfortunate if children's early learning is ignored and they are treated as if they arrive in school with no previous experience to build on. In fact, in National Curriculum terms, their 'knowledge about language' may be considerable.

For instance, many school-age children will already be adept users of their first language and will bring this knowledge to learning a second language. They will know, intuitively, that a language is made up of separate words and has a special word order and grammar. They will recognize, and be able to carry out, language functions such as: greeting people; holding conversations; asking questions. They will be able to interpret expressions and gestures.

These skills can be used if teachers employ such techniques as:

- positioning children where they can see demonstrations of art, craft, music, dance, PE, and can appreciate clear body language and intonation which accompany instructions ('Come here' ... 'Sit down' ... 'Give it to me' ... 'Watch carefully').
- Learning to say 'What's the name for'...? in Punjabi/Urdu etc. 'How do you say 'Good Morning' / 'Please' / 'Thank you' in Arabic/Pushtu?' 'In English we say ... How do you say it in ...?' (This gives an opportunity for teachers to learn something of the languages of their children.)

Such phrases encourage children to make comparisons between languages, to devise rules and infer meanings.

Finally, some languages are closely related to English in terms of vocabulary or grammatical structure or both. Such relationships help children to guess informatively, particularly if the two languages share words with a similar sound (e.g. cognates such as 'telefono'/'telephone' in Spanish/English; 'ball'/'ball' in German/English), or if the languages have borrowed from each other (e.g. French has borrowed 'week-end' and 'parking' from English; English has borrowed 'mosque', 'cotton', 'sofa', 'magazine' from Arabic).

CLASSROOM STRATEGIES

At first, progress may be imperceptible. However, when teachers look back over several months of a child's being in school, they realize how much has been achieved.

One strategy on its own will not do the trick. Several need to be used together gradually to increase a child's confidence and ability. All are incremental.

1 Peer group support

Some of the strategies already mentioned can be thought of as cognitive. More important, perhaps, are social strategies, because these come from a strong motivation to communicate. For this reason, children join groups and act as if they know what is going on; they give the impression, by using the little they know, that they understand more; they make friends and turn to them for help. Children who want to interact with others need language to do so.

Thus, the cognitive strategies, such as inferring meanings and formulating rules, feed off these social interactions. Teachers can support this process by:

- finding someone sociable and helpful to befriend new children and initiate them into classroom and playground routines;
- sitting them with others who are articulate and sociable and who, perhaps, share the same first language;
- ensuring that they often work in collaborative groups and pairs, particularly on activities that require a lot of simple repetitive language or where communicative language can hardly be avoided.

In this regard, the following may be recommended:

- Playing board games (home-made and commercial), such as Lotto, Guess Who, Operation, Dominoes, and card games such as Snap, Pelmanism;
- building construction and Lego models;
- modelling and painting in art and craft;
- making and using puppets;
- playing with sand and water;
- sorting and classifying objects and pictures (animals, vehicles, shapes, furniture, food etc.);
- using telephones and learning different dialogues for different situations;
- playing with model houses, garages, villages, people;

- using role play areas, (hospital, shop, office), and social situations;
- dressing up and acting in improvised plays;
- making and listening to sound effects and playing Sound Lotto;
- using a surprise box, identifying objects by touch and feel;
- miming games and language and playground games, such as modified versions of I Spy, Twenty Questions, Mr Wolf, etc.;
- sequencing picture stories;
- trying out computer games and word processing.

2 A language syllabus

The syllabus suggested here is an amalgam of what are termed 'communicative' and 'task-based' approaches.

Much of what has been said above concerns particular management techniques which will support children's acquisition of English. Teachers will also, when possible, want to do some direct teaching of English. The best opportunities derive from the children's situation in school. To make use of this, teachers must ask themselves: 'What are this child's needs at this moment?' 'What English can this child learn from this particular situation?'

Some needs that can be anticipated are as follows:

(a) On arriving in school children will need to know:
- simple greetings and politeness formulas ('Hello', 'Good morning', 'Thank you', 'Please', 'My name is ...')
- the names of the classroom objects they use ('table', 'chair', 'desk', 'pencil', 'rubber', 'paper', 'book' ...)
- simple commands and routines ('Come here', 'Sit down', 'Have you got a. ..?' 'Line up', 'Tidy up', 'I need a ...', 'I've finished', 'I've lost my ...' 'Can I go to the toilet?')

It helps children to learn if:
- the meaning is made clear through translation, appropriate gestures, the actions of other children, or the use of real objects or good pictures;
- teachers monitor their own language, teach the phrases they actually use, repeat them consistently, but avoid broken English.

(b) Certain items are very easy to teach, because they can be readily demonstrated in a real context. Amongst these are:
- possessives, ('Whose is this?' 'It's mine/yours/his/hers.')
- prepositions, ('Where's your ...?' 'On/in/outside/inside/under/by.')

- states ('I'm hot/cold/tired/hungry/sick/angry.')

(c) Each part of the curriculum helps to introduce and consolidate new language. These areas include:
   - PE: action verbs, commands, adverbs. ('Get changed. Run, jump, bend, balance. Quietly, slowly, quickly. Stop. Stand still. Find a space.')
   - Maths: numbers, colours, processes ('Add. Take away. Equals.') comparisons: ('big/small, bigger/smaller than, tall/short, long, heavy/light'.)

(It is interesting and important here to remember that many children will not be learning these as new concepts; they will actually be re-naming in English.)

   - Reading/Writing: 'Book. Page. Word. Turn over. Back. Front. Top. Bottom. Copy. Draw. Can you say ...? Do you know ...? What's in the picture?'
   - Topics. Each one brings in new vocabulary. Bilingual children can carry out many of the same activities as monolingual children, so long as they understand the purpose. At the same time, they can make their own topic booklets with simple, repetitive sentences to help reinforce reading and writing skills.
   - Stories/songs/rhymes. Especially those with repeated refrains. These can be tape-recorded for group reading, photocopied and used for sequencing, sentence and word-matching, sentence-completion, and book-making. Many old favourites can be used in this way: *The Gingerbread Boy; Are You My Mother? Brown Bear, Brown Bear; The Dark, Dark House; The Enormous Turnip; How Do I Put It On? The Elephant and the Bad Baby.*

Every curriculum area is rich in language. When carrying out National Curriculum forecasting, it may help to include the language items to be taught as well as activities planned.

3 Beginning reading and writing

Teachers are naturally anxious that children develop literacy skills as soon as possible. However, there must be no undue pressure for them to do so. Literacy skills must be developed in tandem with oral skills. There is no point in children reading and writing things they do not understand. Therefore, one of the best ways to start is for the children to make their own books. As well as the topic booklets mentioned before, children can be helped to produce a series of books based on simple repeated sentence patterns which also introduce useful vocabulary, such as:

- A Book about Me
- A Book about My Family
- A Book about My School
- A Book about My Street
- A Book about My Friends
- A Book about My Teacher.

These books can be sent home for parents to read and talk over with the child. The text can be copied, cut up, and used for re-reading and writing, as outlined previously.

At some point, however, teachers will want to use commercially produced materials. Many of the same criteria apply here as apply to selecting any reading material for the classroom. Once again there must be a strong link with meaning.

There should be a good relationship between illustrations and text so that children understand what is going on, or they will simply 'parrot' read. Teachers will want to avoid books that present unfamiliar or inappropriate cultural situations, racial or gender stereotypes, archaic or idiomatic English. This may mean being very selective in choosing books available from school and local libraries.

Some children will have attended school in another country and may already be fluent readers and writers. Since they have acquired those concepts associated with literacy (such as, that print conveys meaning; that there is a relationship between symbols and sounds), it is obviously easier for them to transfer this knowledge to reading and writing in English. If the first language is written in Roman script this transfer will be even more straightforward. For literate children, books and stories can provide a very useful way to begin learning a new language, and, of course, they should continue to read in the first language.

As far as specific techniques go, teachers can:

(a) Enlist the aid of parents or other communicators to help children make their own dual-text dictionaries or phrase books.
(b) Make alphabet or phonic books with a sound on each page. Children can cut out or draw objects to illustrate the sound. In some languages there is a direct relationship between sounds and symbols. This is not always the case in English.
(c) Acquire materials in the appropriate language. Many libraries and bookshops now have a range of dual-text and foreign-language books, dictionaries and phrase books.

(d) Contact EFL publishers who produce specialist courses for overseas (notably: Oxford University Press, Cambridge University Press, Longman, Collins). While teachers will not want to purchase a whole course, the accompanying workbooks are often very useful for providing progression and directing teachers to the language items they can focus on.

(e) Use appropriate handwriting materials. Children may have learnt a script which does not have a left-to-right orientation. Handwriting patterns will help them to practise Roman script.

(f) Develop a language awareness topic with the whole class. Collect examples of scripts and information about languages. Encourage the bilingual children to bring in examples of written materials, to write the names of their classmates, to add to classroom labels. Parents can be invited in to talk about their school-days and their language.

Part 1: Languages we know (questionnaire for discussion or writing)

My name is ....

1 Here is the word for HELLO in my language...

2 I know the names of these languages...

3 I have heard people speaking these languages ....

4 I speak to my mum in ....

5 I speak to my dad in...

6 I speak to my brother named ....in ....

7 I speak to my sister named ....in ....

8 I speak to my grandfather in ....

9 I speak to my grandmother in ....

10 When I play games at home I speak...

11 When I watch TV I speak ....

12 In class at school I speak..

13 Inside my head I speak ....

14 In my dreams the people speak ....

15 I can read in ....

16 I can count in ....

17 I go to language classes after school. Yes / No

18 I go to language classes at the weekend. Yes / No

19 A language I would like to learn is ....

20 Here is the word for GOODBYE in my language...

What did you learn about yourself from answering these questions?

Part 2: What I feel about languages

My name is ....

1 It is important to learn other languages because ....

2 It would / would not be a good idea for everyone in the world to speak the

   same language because...

3 I like the sound of these languages..

4 I don't like the sound of these languages ....

5 Some languages are more useful than others because ....

6 No language is better than another. True / False. Why?.....................................

7 A person whose voice I like is named ....

8 I like the sound of his / her voice because ....

9 A language I think would be easy to learn is..

10 I think it would be easy to learn this language because....................................

11 Talking / Reading / Writing. Which is the most useful? Why?

12 Everybody should learn more than one language. True / False. Why?

What did you learn about yourself or about languages from answering these
questions?

Note: Further questionnaires may be devised to explore accent and dialect.

Chapter 2

A young child learns English
Sukhwant Kaur and Richard Mills

EDITORS' INTRODUCTION

The famous words of the Plowden Report (1967) – 'At the heart of the educational process lies the child' – remain powerful and relevant, albeit tempered now by a stress on skills and assessment. Bilingual education reflects this balance. Valuing and building on mother tongue derives from a child-centred philosophy, but is also in keeping with the notion of skill development. Accordingly, this chapter analyses the English learning process experienced by one young boy, in the belief that we can discover as much, if not more, by such scrutiny, as by many a larger survey.

Lacking English, 5-year-old Jasdeep uses his senses of sight, touch, smell and hearing to learn from his teacher, his peers, his classroom experiences. He imitates the behaviour of his classmates in a fairly unselective way. As a confident, extrovert Punjabi speaker, who is prepared to make mistakes, he already has advantages over less confident, introverted, tentative people. Evidence suggests (see McDonough, 1981) that those learners who make good progress are often risk-takers, striving to communicate by means of the little language they possess.

Jasdeep's teacher needs to practise all manner of visual/verbal/body language strategies; to involve him in a variety of peer groupings and practical experiences; to make judicious use of repetition and ritual. She needs to show that both Jasdeep and his first language are valued; that she is prepared to surrender some of her teacher authority in promoting a language she herself does not understand; that she will tolerate minor short-term indiscipline for what she hopes will be a longer-term good.

So there are many messages here for monolingual teachers in multilingual classrooms. They include the need for:

- close observation of individual children;

- a level of empathy by which we do our utmost to get inside the mind of the child;
- a realization that second-language acquisition, like learning to read, is a slow process, not to be instantly achieved by the wave of a magic wand;
- a balance between repetition of certain frequently occurring language structures, and a more open-ended context in which freer language may flourish;
- a preparedness to live with error and misunderstanding, as the inevitable prelude to greater accuracy, both in English usage and mother tongue interpretation.

Here, then, is a tiny glimpse into the world of Jasdeep, the pupil, and Miss Evans, the teacher.

Teacher: Now, children, you know we only have four in the home corner.

Child: I am four.

Jasdeep is a 5-year-old, Punjabi-speaking, Sikh boy, who was born in India and attended school there for three months, before coming to England with his mother and older sister to join his father and older brothers. He now lives in a well-established multi-ethnic community in a large city suburb and attends a primary school built in the nineteenth century. The school has some 280 children, aged 4–11 years, who are largely Punjabi speakers (i.e. 67 per cent as a first language), but interspersed with first-language speakers of Bengali (7 per cent); English (18 per cent); Gujerati (1 per cent); Mirpuri (1.5 per cent); Pushtu (0.5 per cent); Urdu (5 per cent).

My observations of Jasdeep were of the non-participant, unstructured kind, and lasted some twenty-five hours in all, over ten sessions. They involved: note-taking; tape recording and transcribing; conducting tests; discussion with children (in Punjabi largely) and with teachers (in English); maintaining a retrospective journal.

What follows now is a set of extracts from my series of observations, with interpretations I made at the time. In particular, I was interested to see:

- how Jasdeep was adjusting to classroom life;
- how other children reacted to him;
- how the teacher catered for his special needs in classroom activities.

The observations concern the following activities:

- cooking jacket potatoes;
- making a pattern for Divali with coloured sticky paper;
- participating in a whole-class PE lesson, using large apparatus;
- using calculators in a number lesson.

COOKING JACKET POTATOES

Jasdeep joins in with the class of twenty-seven boys and girls to say, 'Good afternoon everyone'. During registration, he repeats those names which the teacher emphasizes. It seems as though he is very sensitive to intonation. He answers, 'Yes Miss Evans', when his name is called during registration. This is a time of much repetition and a routine which occurs at least twice every day, and this may explain why Jasdeep is aware of the expected behaviour norms. When asked to stand in line, Jasdeep is not sure of where to go in the classroom, so the teacher asks Michael to guide him into the line and Michael does this by physically moving him. Jasdeep pushes his way into line, jumping the queue. The group walks in a line to the staffroom kitchen for cookery.

The teacher's intention is to involve the children in a series of cookery lessons in order to develop certain mathematical concepts (such as measuring, weighing, estimating, comparing); certain science concepts (such as those to do with change, condensation, heat); certain language concepts (as expressed in vocabulary and structures). Today, the children are to cook jacket potatoes.

When the teacher asks who eats jacket potatoes at home, Jasdeep, like the other children, puts his hand up straight away and says, 'Miss! Miss!' in imitation of the others. However, I suspected that Jasdeep probably did not eat jacket potatoes at home and later asked his mother about this. She confirmed my suspicion. So it would seem that some of the things Jasdeep says and does are merely in imitation of other children, and this is how much of his learning may take place.

As soon as any participation is called for, Jasdeep, like the others, puts his hand up and says, 'Miss! Miss!' even though he clearly does not understand what is involved. He simply copies other children's examples. He is very reliant upon first-hand experience and the use of his senses. The teacher acknowledges this and says, 'Let Jasdeep touch it, too'. Jasdeep then handles the potato and looks around at the other children and at what they are doing and how they are responding. He appears very dependent upon other children to pick up clues as to how to behave. He needs to know how to interpret and make use of the evidence of his senses within this particular school context. The experience alone is not sufficient; he must know what to do with it, within his peer group. It would seem that the method of teaching which will most help him achieve this needs to be very visual and practical.

Jasdeep smells a baked potato and pulls a face that his partner finds rather amusing. It seems that an instinctive reaction to something which is unfamiliar or strange is to laugh.

Miss Evans asks the bilingual Punjabi speakers in the class:

T:	What's the word for soft?
Child 1:	Soft *heh*. (It's soft – uses English word, 'soft'.)
Child 2:	*It's very hot.*
T:	How do you say, 'It's hard?'
Child 2:	*Bohth* hard *heh*. (It's very hard – uses English word, 'hard'.)
T:	Oh it's the same word in Punjabi. Is it?

(NB This is not so but one can easily see how Miss Evans came to this conclusion. The monolingual person, child or teacher, is disadvantaged in such a context.)

Speakers of languages other than English can often be handicapped by the inability to initiate conversation or volunteer their own thoughts and suggestions in English. Instead they have to wait until they are invited into conversations and events. They are primarily receivers of information and rarely have the opportunity to offer understandable oral contributions. Do they consequently feel a sense of failure, inadequacy or frustration, or do they simply come to accept a passive role within such a context?

Jasdeep laughs when the other children laugh at the idea, suggested by one child, of potatoes looking like frog's toes, even though he doesn't understand the joke. This is another indication that Jasdeep's behaviour is based largely on imitation. He has to appear to conform to peer group expectations. Many a teacher could be misled by such conformity into believing that he really does understand what is being said.

During the cooking Jasdeep appears very curious and reaches forward to get closer to the baked potatoes. The other children move forward to smell the baked potatoes and Jasdeep immediately takes this as an indication that he can do the same.

T:	Jasdeep, can you see the wet under the potatoes?

Jasdeep is being involved, but does he really understand what is being asked of him? Perhaps instead he should have been encouraged to touch the condensation created by the steam from the baked potatoes. After all, the question in isolation probably meant very little to him and, in touching the water, he could have been left with an experience to think about.

Evidently, there are times when it is inappropriate for teachers to assume that speakers of languages other than English will necessarily benefit from direct involvement and questioning, and knowing what is appropriate in particular circumstances is a skill which can only come with experience. Sometimes it may be more appropriate to ask a child who has full command of English to lead the activity, thereby requiring the non-speaker to take a secondary role and be more gently absorbed into the event.

When the teacher asks the bilingual Punjabi speakers the word for 'steam', they reply, *'dhouhahn'* (Punjabi for 'smoke' when, in fact, the Punjabi for steam is actually *'pahf'*).

Children often convey incorrect information to the teacher and the amount of Punjabi that some of the younger generations of bilingual children possess is becoming increasingly diluted. In the light of this, the extent to which the teacher can rely on the accuracy of their translation is decreasing. After all, in some of the lines quoted above, the bilingual Punjabi speakers have actually used the English version of the word most important to the sense of the sentence. In spite of this, the children do have good intentions and are eager to assist both Jasdeep and the teacher.

Jasdeep also copies the body language of the other children and when the teacher asks for the help of two sensible children, like the others, he, too, puts his finger on his lips and sits 'nicely'.

The children tell the teacher that the Punjabi for 'hot' is *'thuthah'* and the Punjabi for cold is *'dhundah'*, and this is perfectly right. Jasdeep understands these terms and repeats them. Because two of the words fundamental to an understanding of the lesson have been translated for Jasdeep's benefit, he has, at least, learnt something from the session. In such a way, even limited knowledge, when precisely applied, can be helpful.

Miss Evans then involves Jasdeep by asking him to cut the baked potato and hands him a knife. He succeeds in this task. This may be because the instrument he has been given indicates what he must do with it. Here is an example of how context-based activities and situational clues can assist learning.

Speakers of other languages appear extremely reliant on eye-contact, the teacher's gestures and contextual clues to deduce what is required of them and so it is vital to provide these pupils with such clues at regular intervals throughout the lesson, by building such considerations into lesson planning. The need for context-based learning becomes crucial in the case of non-English speakers. By wanting to learn from the children, the teacher indicates that she values the languages of her children. However, the incorrect information that is sometimes passed to her illustrates how precarious the situation is for the monolingual teacher in a multilingual classroom (or, indeed, for the bilingual teacher who does not share the same languages as her bilingual pupils).

Miss Evans cuts half of a baked potato into quarters. Jasdeep is unsure as to whether he should follow this example and asks some other children what to do. They are equally uncertain and so he hesitates. At this point the teacher instructs him to cut the half in half again. Jasdeep immediately obliges, realizing that his own original inclination was right.

From the point of view of mathematics, the Cockcroft Report (1982) stresses the importance of assisting learning via 'means of activities and discussion in the classroom'. As the latter may not always be possible with speakers of other languages, it means that the necessity of learning through practical activity is of even greater importance. It is important to incorporate a lot of practical activity into the child's programme of work to maintain his sense of interest and achievement at times when a lack of language understanding may make him feel isolated or non-motivated.

Jasdeep puts some butter on his baked potato. He is unsure of how to hold his fork, so he watches another girl and follows her example. A girl shows him her potato. She says, 'Look.' He smells it and says, 'Ugh!' Jasdeep then says, 'Miss my finished.' He is now beginning to communicate and initiate conversation in English. On such occasions, the teacher could praise and reinforce children's oral contribution by repeating what has been said and saying something like, 'Jasdeep has finished' and then saying, 'X has finished. Y has finished'. However, the teacher cannot assume sudden language development and proceed to bombard the child with a succession of overwhelming further questions.

There is some evidence, in fact, that even in monolingual classrooms, teachers ask hundreds of questions each day, thereby limiting the scope for time and reflection by children attempting to respond. The certainty that supplementary questions will follow an answer, as surely as night follows day, may act as a disincentive for children to answer in the first place.

On the whole, Jasdeep is relatively quiet. The obvious explanation is that this is because he lacks English, though we must not dismiss the fact that he is able to talk fluently in Punjabi. However, the way Jasdeep's eyes constantly scan what is going on, and what the other children are doing, suggests that his silence is due to the concentration involved in picking up any available contextual clues. A girl leans back and yawns; Jasdeep imitates this. Similarly, when a boy jumps up and down on his chair, Jasdeep does the same.

It seems that he emulates the behaviour of other children, regardless of whether it is acceptable or not. The teacher must, therefore, be wary of rebuking a child for negative behaviour which may actually have been copied from another child. After all, if the children's initial learning takes place through oral and physical imitation, then it may be difficult for them initially to discriminate between acceptable and non-acceptable behaviour. They may either lack the criteria by which to judge what is acceptable or they may act on different criteria.

While the other children tidy up, at the end of cookery, Jasdeep keeps running in and out of the kitchen area. He then rubs his hands clean on a sponge far more energetically than is necessary. Perhaps this excess of physical expression, not uncommon in many childen, is a release of pent-up energy that he has been unable to channel through full intellectual and oral involvement in the lesson. Or, perhaps, it is simply a settling-down period that he must gradually go through.

THE CASE OF THE DIVALI CANDLES: AN ART AND CRAFT LESSON, WITH STICKY PAPER

On another occasion, the class is involved in a different practical activity. The teacher has distributed to each child three pieces of coloured sticky paper (blue, red, yellow), glue and scissors. The children are to put the papers on top of each other and cut out a self-chosen shape. The six resulting pieces of paper will then be arranged in a pattern. The activity is designed to exercise manipulative, fine motor skills in cutting and sticking, and creativity in the arrangement of symmetrical shapes using various colours to produce a pleasing design.

Jasdeep sits on his chair in the classroom and fidgets with the glue, unaware as yet of the task. He is very eager to have the right items in front of him. While Miss Evans demonstrates what is to be cut and how, Jasdeep sits opening and closing the scissors in his mouth. He then moves to the opposite side of the table and now has his back to the teacher. He has obviously not chosen the most advantageous place to seat himself and it would be better for him to sit in a position where he has a good view of what the teacher is doing.

All the time his eyes are scanning the other children to see how they are working. He takes much delight in what he has cut out and shows the teacher, who praises his effort. He glues down what appear to be some leaves and leaf templates that he has just cut out. He shows the teacher his work and she says, 'Oh they look like leaves. Well done,' and writes his name on his picture. The teacher then asked me to ask Jasdeep what he had done and he said, '*Moh buhthiahn*' (which means 'candles'). I asked him what one part was and he replied, '*Ahgh*' (which means 'fire') and when I asked him what another part was, he said, '*Moh buhthiahn*' ('candles'). For him, and all the other children, the open-ended art activity has been narrowed down into a production of Divali candles.

Jasdeep uses three colours of gummed paper and matches the corresponding colour of flame on the same colour of candle. Interestingly, although Jasdeep does not know the name of the colours 'blue' and 'red' in Punjabi, he does know them in English and this causes one to question the appropriateness of testing certain concepts in Punjabi if children have not been taught them in their first language. After all, Jasdeep only knows the names of these two colours because he has been taught them in English in a British school. This is why the National Curriculum needs to clarify the circumstances in which children could be tested through mother tongue. (More of this later in the book.)

I asked him when candles are lit in India. He answered, 'Divali' and began to tell me about fireworks. Here is an occasion when, because the child is not able to correct the teacher's assumptions about his work, his intentions are misinterpreted. Having access to the child's language enabled me to initiate and extend conversation with Jasdeep and discuss exactly what he had made. The teacher who does not understand the child's mother tongue cannot experience such an encounter, and this must be a great barrier and cause of frustration to all concerned.

A PE LESSON

The whole class uses large apparatus. Having observed Jasdeep in a small-group, staff-kitchen context, and during a practical classroom activity, I was particularly keen to follow him and his classmates for PE in the school hall. How would he respond in the larger setting where, because of the range of apparatus and movement, he might have more difficulty in matching teacher instructions to specific observed activity? In such a context, what response would he make to Miss Evans' instructions? What I was hoping to explore was how speakers of other languages cope with a task that is heavily dependent upon an understanding of English, and to what extent they are dependent upon imitating their peers.

The children took it upon themselves to make sure that everyone was getting changed and one child declared, 'Jasdeep change!' However, Jasdeep did not comply. I asked him what the other children were doing and he told me that they were removing their clothes. So he was aware of what the others were doing but decided not to follow their example, saying he did not want to get changed. Perhaps he did not know that the rule also applied to him or perhaps he was not totally at ease with the idea of taking his clothes off at school. Many a school ritual is baffling to the uninitiated, of whatever language background.

T: Get changed. Come along!

Another child helps Jasdeep to get changed.

Jasdeep shows the teacher a flower pattern and says, 'Flower'. The teacher helps him with his clothes. At first, he seems uncertain, but after some attention from Miss Evans, he gets changed. He seems pleased with himself and shows me that he is changed. He then tiptoes around.

At registration Jasdeep repeats another child's name (Henry) in English a number of times.

T: Is everyone in line?

T rebukes a child. All the children quieten down and Jasdeep tells me, 'Naughty boy ah' ('he is a naughty boy'). So Jasdeep obviously understands a tone of reproof.

At first he follows me in the hall, and then returns to where the other children are and quietly sits down with them. The teacher explains that they must all stay on their set piece of apparatus.

T: On the climbing frame go up and climb down.

(The teacher uses hand movements to explain her instructions.)

At this point Jasdeep copies the other children and, putting his hand up, calls, 'Miss! Miss!' He then copies her arm movements as she explains what the children are to do. Lots of different instructions are relayed which must be incomprehensible to him.

T: Jasdeep's group go to the ...

(The teacher points to the piece of apparatus in question.)

This is an excellent way of indirectly guiding Jasdeep, because the use of his name at the beginning of the sentence indicates that the instructions are applicable to him. Jasdeep immediately knows that this set of instructions concerns his group, and, having already heard other names called out and seen children get up and sit by various pieces of apparatus, he knows what he and his group are expected to do. Also being in a group means that, if he is not entirely sure of what to do, he would still be able to follow the others.

Jasdeep leans over a piece of apparatus, whilst the teacher is talking.

T: Get down off the apparatus for a minute.

(Jasdeep rolls off.)

T: When I clap my hands, stop and change over. One at a
                time.

(Jasdeep puts his hand up. Then he joins in the activity and manages to roll well but gets over-excited.)

T: This group are being silly. (Jasdeep's group.)

Jasdeep climbs on a different piece of apparatus, contrary to the teacher's instructions that the children should stay on their own piece of apparatus. When she raises her voice to the rest of the class, he quickly joins his own group. Jasdeep runs over to Miss Evans, smiling. She sends him back. Copying the action of his other group members, he does not move along the apparatus one at a time. He is misled by emulating the improper actions of others and sometimes gets told off for doing so. In a sense, Jasdeep is at the mercy of other children's behaviour. For example, when they get excited and misbehave, he may have little choice but to follow their example.

T: Right on the mat!

(Jasdeep does not go back to his group starting-point, but runs out to the mat on the opposite side of the apparatus and flops on it.)

T: Jasdeep, show us what you did.

(Jasdeep demonstrates his roll.)

T: Jasdeep is going in and out.

In such a way, he is singled out for recognition.

PE has the potential to facilitate language learning, because achieving the desired physical response is heavily dependent upon language understanding, and the language used to describe the actions is embedded in the action itself. Understanding the words and their associations is assisted by the context. The teacher talks the other children through Jasdeep's actions and this is a good way of supplying speakers of other languages with the vocabulary necessary to explain their own movements. However, it is not always possible or appropriate to talk through everything children do. After all, if the speakers of other languages are not doing what is required, it may not always be possible to use them as examples and thereby provide them with task-related language.

Miss Evans points to where Jasdeep's group should go to next and asks them to sit down. No-one obeys. On the next piece of apparatus, Jasdeep often moves out of line and climbs on the wrong piece. When confronted by many sets of instructions, Jasdeep is uncertain about which cues to follow. At one point, he simply crouches down on the mat and watches a number of other children, perhaps in an attempt to work out if their behaviour has something in common that he should copy, and whose behaviour to copy.

T: Jasdeep, can you jump in and out?

(Jasdeep fails to understand the instruction.)

T: Samina, can you explain?
S: *Jasdeep* jump *in car*!

(Child uses English version of verb.)

Here the limited Punjabi of the interpreter means that the most import-ant words in the sentence that convey the desired action are not translated.

At first Jasdeep takes no notice, so, by having always to communicate via a third person, some of the teacher's immediate authority is lost. She then repeats the instruction and physically assists Jasdeep to do what she has asked him.

T: Come off the apparatus and sit down.

However, Jasdeep continues jumping up and down and climbing in and out of the apparatus.

Miss Evans then calls his name in a disapproving tone and Jasdeep gets off the apparatus. He does not yet fully understand the importance of immediately obeying instructions, particularly in PE where the safety factor is paramount. Perhaps, because he lacks the language and relies on watching the rest of the class to deduce what he must do, it means that, when he is engrossed in his own activity to the point that he forgets to look around him, he fails to realize that the rest of the class are obeying a new set of instructions and it subsequently appears that he is being disobedient. There is an inevitable time-lag between instruction and response. Equally, there is a need to safeguard against the danger of the child believing that different kinds of behaviour are acceptable.

Jasdeep is very good on the climbing frame, and PE, like certain other activities, is an area in which children who do not initially have full command of the language necessary for academic success can excel and prove their worth.

T: You're taller than me now.

(T says this using hand movements to indicate height. It is another example of the potential for language development in PE, potential which particularly applies in the areas of movement, measurement, command, position.)

Jasdeep runs off into the wrong group, wanders around, and then returns to his own group again.

Three specific implications strike me after observation of this PE lesson:

- One of the disadvantages of being heavily dependent on others is that such children are less likely to produce anything original. Teachers may, on this account, underestimate a child's creativity.
- There is a definite need to integrate the learning programme of speakers of other languages within mainstream class work. In such a context, social development occurs naturally, alongside language learning.
- As an observer, I must acknowledge that some of Jasdeep's running around and jumping up and down may have been done to attract my attention, as he appeared to know that I was interested in him. No researcher can ever collect data (legally/morally) without affecting the situation in some way.

At the end of the session, Jasdeep lines up with the rest of the class.

T: When you've got changed sit on the carpet.

Jasdeep immediately gets changed and follows the example of the other children.

A NUMBER LESSON USING CALCULATORS

Jasdeep is sitting in a group of eight children with Miss Evans. They are becoming familiar with calculators and using them to reinforce number recognition. Jasdeep is sharing a calculator with Samina.

S (Samina):   Miss, you do it like this.

S offers Jasdeep the following instructions in Punjabi:

S: *Press this. Twice. You have to go up to a hundred.*

Pointing to the numbers on his calculator, I ask Jasdeep:

SK: *What are these?*
J: Number.

(Jasdeep keeps pressing the '=' sign on his calculator. Samina shows him how to get '55555555' to appear on his calculator. I ask him how many there are. He asks Samina.)

S: *A lot. A lot. A million.*

(S then presses '2695' on her calculator.)

S: This is less.

T: You've got some numbers. Have you? What numbers
                 have you got?

(T says the numbers aloud. Jasdeep repeats them.)

T: Everyone clear your calculators.

(Samina shows and tells Jasdeep how to clear his calculator. Jasdeep
follows instructions.)

T: Good boy Jasdeep. I'm going to draw round this triangle.
                 Tell me a number.

(Jasdeep quickly puts his hand up. He looks happy and sits rocking on his
chair. Meanwhile the teacher has put the number '8' in the triangle that
she has drawn.)

T: Now I'm going to put some numbers in the corners to
                 add up to eight. If I put four there, how many more do I
                 need?

First some children say eight, then four. Meanwhile Samina is doing
Jasdeep's work for him rather than simply assisting him to do it himself.
For example, Jasdeep presses '4' and then the '+' sign twice instead of just
once. Instead of correcting him, Samina takes over. The other children
work independently, whereas Samina and Jasdeep share the one calculator.

S: Jasdeep, eight.
J: Eight.

(Jasdeep appears to be learning by rote.)
    I ask Jasdeep what number it is. He repeats exactly what Samina says,
which is, 'One, two, three, four', and then shows me five fingers.
    Generally the teacher was looking at, and talking to, Samina in her role
as interpreter and not to Jasdeep. In this respect, having an interpreter can
be a hindrance, allowing the teacher to bypass the need to communicate
with the child himself.
    The teacher draws a triangle. I ask Jasdeep what it is.

J: *It flies up.*

(Perhaps he thinks it is an aeroplane. He certainly does not realize that it
is called a 'triangle'.)

T: Jasdeep, draw round the triangle.

(T puts the triangle in front of Jasdeep.)

How does Jasdeep know what to draw round if he does not know that it is called a 'triangle'? Perhaps on hearing the word, he recognizes what it represents, because of the object/word correspondence and contextual clues, whereas if shown the object and then asked to say its name, he is unable to. This would be a possibility, since, as Donaldson (1987) says, where aided by contextual clues, language 'comprehension precedes production'.

T asks to borrow his triangle. Jasdeep gives it to her. Jasdeep picks up the calculator, Samina says, 'No'.

Jasdeep copies Teacher's number '3'. Shows me his number '3'. Appears pleased with it. Smiles.

His eyes are constantly wandering. Miss Evans does not question Jasdeep on the actual task. He seems almost oblivious of the fact that the teacher is actually speaking. As Miss Evans converses with other children, Jasdeep goes over his number '3' several times. He does not join in with the conversation, but doodles. As soon as the other children begin to do something, he writes, copying from Samina. Every time understanding is called for, Jasdeep relies on his partner. When I ask him what number was in the middle of his triangle, he looks at Samina and, on her advice says, 'Three'.

So, it seems he is reliant on his interpreter not only for communication, but also for understanding and for answers. Is this a desirable way of learning and does it provide the teacher with accurate feedback on Jasdeep's understanding? The appropriateness of interpreting at this level is questionable. Is it against Jasdeep's best interests, or is it merely a staging-post which he needs to pass through until his own language competence develops? With some pairings, and in some circumstances, there must be a fine dividing line between collaborative learning on the one hand, and unthinking reliance, on the other. This does not diminish the potential value of pair work, but it does call for professional scrutiny.

T: Jasdeep, what number do you want? Right, six. Keep pressing it till you fill it up. Now count how many sixes you have in the window.

(What has appeared on the calculator is '66666666'. The question that the teacher asks is actually a difficult one to absorb and understand.)

T: Samina, choose another number. An easier one.

Following the example of the other children, Jasdeep puts his hand up, and, like them, calls, 'Miss! Miss!'

Jasdeep can clear his calculator by following Miss Evans' instructions.

T:	See if you can draw number '2' like that. (T points to the '2' on the calculator.)
SK:	You do this like this. (I say this, pointing to the '2' on the calculator. He does it.)
S:	No. Like this.

Samina draws hers more accurately. Now Jasdeep copies her number '2' and not the '1' on the calculator. If Samina were to make an error, so would Jasdeep. Is working in this fashion appropriate?

T:	Do you want to try a different number? Clear it. Clear it.

(Jasdeep just nods his head, so the teacher clears it for him.)

When I questioned Samina, she appeared to understand her role. She said she must report back to the teacher. She says Jasdeep has chosen number '1' but he is, in fact, continuing to draw the number '2'. How does a monolingual teacher check that a bilingual pupil has conveyed correct information to a non-English-speaking partner? Checking retrospectively by results is not foolproof, even if it is understandable, given a class of thirty children.

Miss Evans teaches by demonstration. Jasdeep now has this on his calculator: '111111111.'

T:	Can you do number ones?

Jasdeep copes with the situation by copying. Jasdeep has actually drawn nine ones.

T:	Have you done eight? (She counts them.) There's too many.

T now gives Jasdeep and Samina a number game to play and explains the rules to Samina.

S:	*Jasdeep, we are going to play a game. Do well. Do it properly. Don't do that with your eyes – or else it'll ...*

If the interpreter does not comprehend the task, the speakers of other languages have no chance of understanding. Jasdeep's learning is dependent upon how well Samina understands and transfers the information. Moreover, she has a natural tendency to do things for him. In her eyes it is both quicker and more reliable. In fact, Jasdeep does not have a basic grasp of number. How, then, can he make sensible use of a calculator? He appears to be working hard, but his understanding is minimal.

The teacher asks the rest of the class to sit on the mat. When I asked

Jasdeep what the teacher had said, he replied, *'on the carpet'*. I asked him if he also had to go on the carpet and he said, 'Yes'. I then asked Samina and she said this was not so and now Jasdeep also decided that he did not have to go on the carpet. There is clearly some confusion here. Jasdeep knows he must ask if he can go to the toilet and manages to do this independently. Samina tells me what the teacher has just said to the other children about going out. On her own accord Samina takes responsibility for passing general classroom conduct on to Jasdeep, and when he arrives from the toilet she says, *'Sh! Don't make any noise'*, regardless of the fact that the teacher has not actually requested Samina to pass this information on to Jasdeep.

SUMMARY

How, then, can we facilitate the learning of speakers of other languages? My observations of Jasdeep lead me to certain conclusions.

(a) Successful language learning is aided by genuine contexts. This is most aptly put by Klein (1986): 'the meaning of any word emerges from our knowledge of the situation'. It is illustrated, vividly, by Donaldson (1987), who describes an English woman in the company of an Arab woman and her two children, a boy aged seven and a girl aged thirteen months. Neither group spoke the other's language. The little girl was walking from her mother to the English woman and back again, where-upon the English woman pointed to the boy and said, 'Walk to your brother this time'. The boy, understanding the situation but not the words, held out his arms and the baby walked to him. The meaning of the language in this situation was highly predictable from this context.

Much of Jasdeep's behaviour in the observations described above reflects his recognition of such predictability and an ability to capitalize on this. He appears to make maximum use of his senses – smelling, touching, and testing and observing others. In the PE lesson the language used to describe movements is embedded in the action itself.

The fact that, in cookery, a knife is given to him to cut the potato indicates what he has to do. Likewise, there are several occasions when Jasdeep is able to interpret not only the body language of the teacher and the other children, but also tone of voice, particularly, of course, in relation to inappropriate behaviour.

(b) Repetition and imitation are important strategies. Jasdeep is adept at following classroom routines, such as answering his name and lining up. His quietness, partly due to his lack of English, could have led, in a different school, to his being labelled passive or slow-learning. Swann (1985) speaks of how often we have a negative attitude towards people with limited English and asks us to consider the connotation of referring to them as 'not speaking English' or 'not speaking English properly'. It may also be inappropriately observed that a child who speaks no English has no language. A further explanation for Jasdeep's quietness is that his eyes are constantly scouring the classroom, so that, on occasions, this apparent passivity is attributable to the fact that he is concentrating on picking up any available contextual clues. Consequently, it goes without saying that speakers of other languages need maximum all-round vision. By moving his seat in the art lesson Jasdeep puts himself at a disadvantage.

(c) Mother-tongue support is highly significant. During the cooking lesson the teacher encourages the children to compare words in Punjabi and English. Obviously, knowledge of a few key Punjabi words is an advantage here. Tansley, however, notes that some teachers feel they are not in control of a particular part of the curriculum if children are using languages they do not understand (1986).

However, it can be crucial for young bilingual children to use mother tongue in class not only to emphasize the child's sense of group identity, but also to relieve the pressures of the initial cultural transition from home to school. Recognition of the child's first language is of the utmost importance if there is to be the motivation to progress further. It goes without saying that more bilingual professionals are needed in schools, and as Saunders (1988) stresses, it is important to provide those who need 'to deal with children from bilingual homes with basic, factual information about bilingualism in their training programmes'. Both the issue of supply and that of training are addressed later in this book.

Much of the support Jasdeep receives is via other children, often deliberately chosen to help him. It would, of course, become a burden if the same children are always chosen to give support.

However, in general it appears that being asked to interpret for the teacher is a task which makes bilingual children feel valued as a key asset to the teacher, and, on the whole, they seem to enjoy doing it, a point which is developed in Chapter 6. Moreover, it may be that, if the bilingual child translates correctly, the need to explain something to another child may help to clarify and reinforce the bilingual child's own learning rather than hinder it.

However, it must be remembered that this increase in esteem experienced by the bilingual child is a product of the another child's incomprehension and therefore signifies inadequacy on his/her part. In a sense, having an interpreter can be a hindrance, allowing the teacher to bypass the need to communicate with speakers of other languages, and thereby perhaps delaying the development of a close relationship between teacher and taught.

Bilingual children are often excellent resources and, sometimes, the only assistance available to the teacher. By using pupils as interpreters and wanting to learn from them, the teacher can indicate that she values the children in her class and the languages spoken by them. However, it also puts her very much at the mercy of the children, and the incorrect information that is sometimes passed on reveals how precarious the situation is for the monolingual teacher in a multilingual classroom. The situation is far from ideal and helps to explain why some of the teachers interviewed by Tansley (1986) felt so uneasy about handling mother tongue. Having to communicate via a third person deprives a teacher of immediate authority. The whole issue of child interpreters is addressed in Chapter 6.

It was interesting that, while the rest of the class worked independently, Jasdeep and his bilingual partner shared the one calculator and one wonders whether such a system may hinder the development of a sense of independence in speakers of other languages. Every time understanding was called for, Jasdeep relied on his partner and so it seemed he was dependent on his interpreter, not only for communication, but also for understanding and answers. Such a heavy reliance on another child could have damaging results. Speakers of other languages cannot be selective; everything, including error, is learnt from the interpreter. Which is more damaging – to risk receiving incorrect information or receiving no information at all?

(d) Speakers of other languages need to be integrated into class activities. After all, developing peer-group relationships, socialization skills and a sense of belonging to the whole class, and not merely to the bilingual section, is as important as facilitating the progress of academic learning. Being supported by the whole of the class seems preferable to feeling helplessly over-dependent on one or two selected class members. Cox (1988) states, 'Where bilingual children need help, this should be given in the classroom as part of normal lessons.' There is a definite need to integrate the learning programme of speakers of other languages to take place with the rest of the class, because, simultaneously with the child's language learning, it allows a great deal of social development to take place. However, the value and appropriateness of integrating Jasdeep, for instance into the calculator group, is questionable; and one might ask if Jasdeep's learning is being delayed, because of the pressure of having to fit in with the rest of the class.

(e) Help should be ongoing. Even having acquired a reasonable grasp of English, bilingual children should continue to be given extra support, in ways suggested later in the book. After all, although children may soon become able to use language for communication with peers on a personal level, they may not have come to terms with academic language and this is something that the teacher needs to realize when checking under-standing.

In conclusion, it is clear that there are no short cuts in teaching speakers of other languages, no instant solutions. The process of learning a new language takes time, and when that language is the medium of instruc-tion, it assumes the utmost importance and therefore warrants heavy input. Cox (1988) points out that parents of ethnic minority children 'expect the education system to give their children above all a good command of English as rapidly as possible'. However, for reasons of socialization, the child should as far as possible be involved in class activities. Klein (1986) makes a distinction between spontaneous and guided language learning, and the balancing of the two is the problem faced by many teachers. On occasions, it is simply easiest with some abstract concepts to draw parallels with the child's mother-tongue equi-valents.

Whereas spontaneous learning is more in line with the idea of working in real contexts, and would better suit children too young to be formally tutored in the English language, we are faced with the need rapidly to teach children enough language to enable them to begin formal learning, especially in the light of National Curriculum attainment targets and testing. This issue is addressed in chapters 3, 4 and 5.

Assessment of and through language

Chapter 3

Monolingual teachers assessing bilingual children

Jean Mills

EDITORS' INTRODUCTION

This chapter serves as a general introduction to those which follow and which focus on specific situations. Any assessment is problematic and one could develop this declension by saying: assessment is difficult; oral assessment is very difficult; bilingual assessment is extremely difficult.

The term 'assessment' itself requires definition. Do we mean assessment of abilities, such as maths concepts, by using mother tongue? Or do we mean, the assessment of an individual's language skills in English and in mother tongue? Whichever aspect is chosen, it is still important to examine the basic premises that underlie any assessment, namely, what is 'good practice' in this area? Obviously, in assessing bilingual children, the same issues will occur, but there will be the added complications of cultural relevance; the influence of particular contexts; the nature of children's abilities in their different languages.

Comfort is offered to teachers who do not share the languages of the children they teach. (Such teachers, of course, may, or may not, be monolingual.) Again, the recommendation is 'back to basics', i.e. to call upon those skills of observation and reflection in which most professionals are already adept. Teachers may then note, as part of formative assessment, children's development of language-learning strategies and, in particular, their knowledge about language (KAL). Assessment in these terms ultimately rests on the collection, and interpretation, of apparently chance remarks in a range of situations. As the examples suggest, reflection on such instances increases a teacher's ability to develop insight into children's language repertoire.

Without bilingual skills, teachers are trying to find the best high-jumper by seeing who's good at running.

(Monolingual teacher)

How do we, as primary school teachers, assess oral language? Do we use tick-off categories on checklists? Do we analyse transcripts of tape recordings? Do we monitor with ongoing judgements as the spoken language is uttered? Perhaps we use combinations of all these, but experience over the past twenty years indicates just how difficult the task is. (See Appendices 3 and 4).

Even the Assessment of Performance Unit (APU) surveys during the 1980s, using a fairly structured technique, only attempted to assess 11-year-olds in the primary range, and then within a circumscribed set of categories (viz. Instructing/Directing, Giving and Interpreting Information, Narrating, Describing, Discussing). How much more difficult it is to achieve anything comprehensive across the age and ability range, when children in the same class speak two or three different languages.

This chapter lays down the premises for the case studies which follow. It attempts to give a conceptual framework to the more detailed and specific discussion in those chapters.

Where, then, can bilingual assessment begin if, by that, we mean:

1 the assessment of specific abilities (such as maths or history concepts) through mother tongue; and
2 the more general assessment of a child's linguistic abilities in English and mother tongue?

It begins from the same fundamental premises that good practice for monolingual children should also be good practice for bilingual children, and that basic assessment procedures will be the same for both groups, albeit with different emphases.

Here, then, are some general criteria which apply as much to multilingual, as to monolingual, classrooms.

(a) A good language classroom supports all the languages, varieties and dialects which are spoken in it.

Thus, it may be appropriate for children to compare their local dialect with standard English (as the National Curriculum requires, see AT1, Level 5, e; 6, d); to write explanations of dialect words; to carry out role play in dialect and standard English.

Similarly, children who can write in scripts other than English can use these skills in any investigation of the history of writing and of alphabets.

Likewise in spoken language where, as the Cox Report indicates, the experience of language of bilingual children is 'greater than that of their monoglot peers' and provides 'a focus for discussion about language forms' (1988:58).

b) Assessment of standard English is only one dimension of a child's all-round language abilities. Some children have a very wide linguistic repertoire, made up of several language varieties. The very term 'bilingual'(see the Introduction and Baetens Beardsmore 1986: Chapter 1) may obscure this, since it is often used in a loose and imprecise way to refer to dual-language users in inner-city schools.

In fact, such children may have high-level oracy and literacy skills in two or more languages; or basic command in one language with more developed skills in another; or oral fluency in two languages but selective use of each according to setting (e.g. playground/classroom/home) or function (e.g. personal/academic). Thus, Bourne's definition, 'Bilingualism stands for the alternate use of two languages in the same individual' (1988: pp. 1, 2), is followed by a caveat about assuming the term indicates equal proficiency or that it offers any judgement about the range or quality of a child's linguistic skills.

As the chapter which follows will indicate, some children have abilities which are only apparent in one language. Many of us have had experience of meeting children who are monosyllabic in English but can carry out lengthy and involved conversations in another tongue, or children who are very able in English but who cannot communicate well in their first language. Similarly, some children have abilities which transfer across language boundaries; they can describe, report incidents, tell stories in two languages.

Here, for example, is 6-year-old Shahira composing a story extempore. She started in English and continued in Pushtu:

> He knocked on Number One's door. He said, 'Can I have a glass of water?' They opened it and said, 'Come in.' They thought it was a man, a nice kind man ... *He didn't really want some water. He came in and got the knife and killed her.*

There are obvious implications for the administration of SAT's (Standard Assessment Tasks). My experience of implementing SAT's using bilingual communicators suggests that not all developing bilingual children benefit, either from having those assessment tasks conducted in English, or having them translated into their mother tongue. In each case, the language used needs to be matched appropriately to the child. Such matching depends on the pre-existence of an adequate language profile for individual children. As one bilingual classroom assistant told me:

If they insist on doing these tests in mother tongue, my children would
fail.

Conversely, in this assistant's same school, a non-English-speaking child,
newly arrived in England from Pakistan, was observed desperately trying
to convey through gesture the rationale behind his sorting of a group of
objects. His difficulty was overcome immediately by using Punjabi.

(c) Assessment should be based on refining teachers' skills of observation
and reflection.

This, of course, applies to both monolingual and bilingual professionals. Obviously, those practitioners who understand the children's mother
tongues have the key to greater insight, and Chapter 4 gives some examples of such insights. However, as the chapter also indicates, such
assessment carries risks. How can one ensure that a translation accurately
reflects both the original question and the child's response? How can one
avoid over-optimistic judgements about a child's ability to speak the first
language?

While monolingual teachers are, undeniably, disadvantaged in making
such assessments, they do possess a knowledge of language development
which can be used, as is indicated later.

(d) All children reveal differences in performance. It may alter according
to their mood, their relationship with other speakers, or the setting in
which they perform. This variability is recognized in the National Curriculum English document which asks for 'a range of situations,
audiences, and activities' (1989:13).

For example, here is Ranjit, aged 5, who, in a one-to-one teaching
situation, would often refuse to communicate. On her own, talking to
herself while sorting set rings, she says, 'Circle, circle ... Each Peach Pear
Plum ... I know what you're writing (*balances a ring on her head*) ... Look,
don't fall down ... I'm gonna have the orange ... (*makes a pattern of rings*) ...
two eyes, one nose, a snowman ... It's nearly snowing.'

Similarly, Nazma (aged 7), who was always mute in the presence of a
teacher in school, and who would read her book in English in a whisper
to a friend, was observed chatting and playing happily at break-time, and
at home spoke in Bengali to her family in front of the home–school liaison
teacher. All these details could figure in any language profile of Nazma.
The presence of another language, in her case Bengali, adds a further
dimension to what has been labelled 'differential performance' (Clark
1988).

Let us now consider this concept.

DIFFERENTIAL PERFORMANCE

Several studies have indicated the ways in which children's language competence may be under-estimated. Joan Tough, for example, collected her data on 3-year-olds by recording children in conversation with a chosen companion, observed by an adult. Margaret Clark (1988:46) rightly suggests that certain factors may well have depressed the performance of some of Tough's children. These include:

- the choice of companion (i.e. the personality of each child and the willingness to talk would affect the situation);
- the presence of an adult;
- the confidence of children from different social backgrounds in adapting to a novel situation.

Similarly, Tizard and Hughes (in Clark 1988:56) found that 'working class' children, assessed at nursery school and then at home, while perfectly competent in the familiar domestic setting, had their abilities under-estimated in a more formal context. Possibly, as Wells (1987) and others have suggested, teachers' expectations may be influenced by the social class of their children; may govern the way they interact with different groups; may affect 'how active, forthcoming and competent [the children] appear' (Wood and Wood, in Clark 1988:87). Naturally, all these provisos will apply to bilingual children. In addition, there will be further considerations:

(a) Children are sensitive to the settings in which they use English and in which they use mother tongue. Many children are quite relaxed in using their first language in the playground or for social interchange in the classroom. What may be more difficult is for them to use that language formally or academically, such as greeting parents in assembly and participating in class lessons.

The policy of the school (see Appendix 8) needs to be quite clear on this matter so that children come to know when it is appropriate for them to use mother tongue. Such occasions could be during:

- news time;
- singing songs and rhymes;
- story-telling by older to younger children;
- interviews;
- role play;
- translation of books;
- small-group discussion of tasks.

During these times the boys and girls need positive encouragement. They need to know that their mother tongue has a legitimate role in the curriculum. Such praise may be overtly expressed in words, but could also be evident in facial expressions and body language. There is a view, for instance (see Baker, 1988), that increased and appropriate eye-contact between teacher and children reinforces the use of mother tongue.

For example, a bilingual colleague has expressed disappointment to me that, during her first term in a new school, children would not use their mother tongue at all. Another colleague discovered that children replied in English until she continually reminded them that they could reply in Punjabi. Only after three years in her present post does she find that children now habitually speak to her in mother tongue. Thus, for some children, a favourable context must include the relationship they have developed with a familiar adult. It is not enough to exhort them to speak Punjabi in school and expect an immediate response.

If children do not use their mother tongue when they are encouraged to do so, teachers will speculate on the reasons. Is it because the school has somehow conveyed negative messages? Is it because mother tongue has come to be regarded as the language of home and English as school language? Is it because parents have given particular instructions?

Whatever the reasons, the effect will be that teachers will have a limited view of the abilities of particular children. The effect on the children will be that they are missing opportunities to practise certain skills through mother tongue. This, in turn, may affect their development in English. After all, if a child has no chance to explain a sequence of events in a science activity, perhaps to another child who could translate, the development of this particular language skill may well be delayed.

(b) Certain settings appear particularly to encourage use of mother tongue.

Observation of Reception and Year One children over several weeks identified the following situations as being especially conducive:

- domestic role play;
- imaginative play with models and construction toys;
- pair work, especially when planning or playing a game;
- working with a bilingual student or other adult;
- cooking a familiar dish.

All these seemed to be 'fair' settings in two ways. They were 'fair' in that the use of mother tongue in such situations was appropriate, relaxed and natural; the children were not under pressure. They were 'fair' also in that the children were using language in situations where they were entirely competent and at ease. They could appear at their best.

As all the children observed had been in school a relatively short time, it was not surprising that they used mother tongue most in those contexts which had a strong link with home. Children as young as five began a communication in English when playing in pairs and switched imperceptibly to Punjabi:

Sunny: Let's have a race then, a race with our cars.
Sucheil: This is the baddy's car, this one.

(Thereafter in Punjabi.)

(c) Children reveal different facets of their personality in different languages.

This is true for us all, of course. We are all more confident when speaking one language rather than another. Fear of mistakes can make us appear diffident, hesitant or shy. Familiarity can make us appear extrovert or ebullient. For instance, 6-year-old Sandeep generally appeared sedate, poised and precise in class. However, one day her teacher asked children if they would do their regular news sessions in mother tongue. Sandeep began telling family stories in Punjabi. She spoke about her younger brother and sister (who were elsewhere in the school); about being locked out of the house by the baby; and about granny (well known by the class teacher as a very powerful individual) who, on one occasion as a helper on a school trip, (a visit to Father Christmas), went off with her group of three children to buy a pair of shoes, thereby missing the bus back to school and causing consternation to those in charge. Sandeep's listeners to these traveller's tales were soon helpless with laughter and Sandeep herself became ever more voluble and excited.

It is worth noting evidence which suggests that, unless learners have been using their second languages for several years (four to six years in one study: Cook, 1991), the 'mind is less efficient in an L2, whatever it is doing'. Unless we take care, we may often be expecting children to perform in their weaker language.

(d) Children may appear less competent simply because they cannot name certain attributes in a particular language.

It is not uncommon to encounter young children who can name colours and shapes in English but have not learnt them in mother tongue. In contrast, older children, newly arrived in England from abroad, may have quite a specialized vocabulary in mother tongue and be able to explain mathematical concepts of weight, height, thickness and so on, but be unable to do so in English. This issue is dealt with later in the book.

OBSERVATION AND INTERPRETATION

Obviously, it is ideal if monolingual teachers can call upon bilingual colleagues and aides to assist with assessment. However, what can mono-lingual teachers do when such resources are not available? What relevant skills do we already possess? The answer surely lies in those traditional areas of teacher strengths, namely, the ability to observe, and the ability to reflect on, and interpret, what has been observed.

If we apply this to the multilingual classroom, two further questions arise. What can we observe, given that we may understand little of what we hear? Furthermore, how do we interpret what is taking place before us? In the light of the National Curriculum emphasis on Knowledge About Language, there are at least two interrelated areas which we can both note and comment on. These are:

- evidence of language learning strategies, and
- evidence of what children know about language as a system.

LANGUAGE LEARNING STRATEGIES

If children are developing bilingually, their English is naturally expan-ding all the time and becoming increasingly more precise. Evidence of the development of their language skills is an important aspect of assessment. In what ways might children reveal that they are grappling with an increasing command over English?

They may do so through non-verbal behaviour. Copying others is an important learning strategy, so that children, while appearing silent and passive, may be watching others intently and following their behaviour (as Jasdeep did in Chapter 2). Their eyes may be continually scanning the classroom. They may make friends by smiling and using appropriate gestures, and engage in play, even though they say nothing.

On the other hand, they may reveal that they are monitoring their own language, particularly if we note those instances where a kind of oral re-drafting is taking place. Sometimes there is evidence of a child getting to grips with an unfamiliar grammatical form. Here, for instance, is 5-year-old Manjit simultaneously grappling with possessive, com-parative, interrogative, and second person singular of the verb 'to be'.:

Mine more better than ... my one more better than yours?

Some Language Support teachers keep a log-book at hand in which to note down such instances as these for work on a subsequent occasion. It is the kind of information which can be used by monolingual teachers as part of formative assessment evidence (see Appendices 3 and 4). Some comments relate to structural competence; others to awareness of social conventions; others to sensitivity to context. Hardeep (aged 7), for instance, tries to weedle a knife from another child. Her first, unsuccessful, overture is, 'Please gimme it'. Her next attempt, which does succeed, is, 'Can you please give it?' All such adjustments of tone, delivery, structure, give us clues, both to the development of a child's English and to the knowledge that child possesses about English as a system.

In addition, it is occasionally possible to observe a range of social and cognitive strategies within relatively short exchanges. In the transcript which follows, Jasvir (J) aged 6, keeps up a running commentary, while Richard (R) has a conversation with the teacher (T). Jasvir, whose first language was Punjabi, had been attending school for nine months. The main purpose of the recording had been to preserve Richard's anecdote about his visit, but the fact that, in the background, Jasvir is practising his English (is, in effect, 'jargoning', much as a younger monolingual child might), is far more interesting.

R:	I went to the Zoo and there was loads of animals. There was giraffes. There was baboons.
J:	Baboons, monkeys.
R:	Things like peacocks.
J:	Things like peacocks.
R:	Giraffes, elephants.
J:	(*laughs*) Helephants.
R:	Gerbils.
J:	Gerbils.
R:	Ah! Gerbils. Miss, Miss Dean used to have gerbils.
T:	That's right, and did any of these animals do anything really interesting?
R:	Yeah, well the gerbils were really funny.
J:	It's very funny.
R:	Through the bars.
J:	Through the bars.
R:	The holes in the bars.
T:	And which animal did you like the most, watching the most?
R:	Ermm, I think it was called a miah cat.
J:	Binky one.

T:	Ah! now why did you like that so much, Richard?
J:	I ...
R:	'Cos they let you ... I like them because 'cos we were allowed to sit in there.
J:	Sit in there.
R:	We were allowed to sit on the edge.
J:	Sit on the chair.
R:	And put our feet ... the miah cats don't bite your feet.
J:	Bite your feet.
R:	They let you sit in see.
J:	Settee.
R:	That was the best bit.
J:	Ah! Button feet.
R:	And there were hippopotamuses.
B:	And monkeys.
J:	There was monkeys, lazy things, the great big...

What we have here is evidence that Jasvir is exercising very powerful language-learning strategies which will work in two ways:

1   They increase the likelihood that others will interact with him, socially and cognitively.
2   They enable him to fit new knowledge into the understanding he already has of how languages work.

How might this occur?

Rather than remain a passive observer, Jasvir repeats some of Richard's words and phrases. This serves not only to make him a group member but also to give him practice in making links between the utterances and this particular context (i.e. a conversation about a reported event).

These well-chosen phrases give the impression that Jasvir understands quite a lot of English. This, in turn, would encourage others (especially his peers) to interact with him so that he continually has feedback from his performance. Such interaction increases the range and type of communicative situation he is involved in and this increases his chance of learning English more quickly. Success breeds success.

Jasvir also uses the recurring parts of utterances and this helps him to develop a feeling for the rules of grammar. He conflates two earlier comments and produces his own (final), more developed, summary. He attempts to incorporate new words and phrases into what he already knows. (Thus, 'sit in there' becomes 'sit on the chair'; 'sit in see' becomes 'settee'; 'best bit' becomes 'button feet'.) In such ways, Jasvir is practising prime functions of language, namely to make meaning and to communicate.

KNOWLEDGE ABOUT LANGUAGE

Children's knowledge about language is revealed on a very wide front. When they practise reading we make judgements about their understanding of print conventions; of how to approach books; of phonics; of the relationship between text and illustration. The strategies they use to begin writing give us information about their notions of word formation; of what words actually are; of story conventions and construction.

If we listen carefully enough to children, other features emerge which can be collected as appropriate evidence to chart their linguistic development. Many of these features will, obviously, also be found among monolingual children. Here are some of them.

(A) Children experiment with language

Here is 7-year-old, Punjabi-speaking Vicki describing his Lego model (in English):

> This is the tea-time teller ... if there's no tea-time teller they'd be left hungry and if they didn't have a crane they wouldn't be able to pick the cars up ... this is the broken car picker ... this is my fixing ramp.

These compound nouns – 'tea-time teller', 'broken car picker' – are not only inventive but based on very reasonable hypotheses, considering words such as 'video-recorder', 'floor-polisher'. They are one indication of Vicki's fluency, flexibility and creative use of English.

(B) Children mix languages

Parmajit asks: 'Who's got the scissors?' (*cenchi*). Jagdip says, 'He go drink water' (*pani*). Kamalpreet comments, 'She's chooping (licking) the ice lolly. He's kitching (pulling) it.'

While there may be several possible interpretations of these utterances, all show a flexibility in communicating which, like Vicki's earlier, is a positive sign.

Knowledge of these individual children obviously helped their teacher to categorize the remarks. But what is actually happening? Does the speaker realize that she is using two languages? (This would, in itself, indicate a stage in her language development.) Does the speaker feel that the Punjabi word fits better? (This would suggest a sophisticated response to her own bilingualism.) Or, does the speaker not know the English equivalent and merely uses a Punjabi version to maintain the flow of speech? (This would suggest a feeling for sequence or fluency.)

(C) Children comment on the performance of others

Thus Rita, listening to Harjit, comments that she says 'lello' for 'yellow'. Harpreet, overhearing another child address the teacher familiarly as 'you' indignantly corrects him, 'No, it's not "you". It's "Mrs Rowheath".'

Such examples, collected incidentally from young children, indicate appreciation of pronunciation and modes of address.

(D) Children use language to talk about language

This may seem an obvious thing to say but what is meant is that, with only a little encouragement, quite young children will compare words between languages. This very matching enables them to stand back and realize that words are labels, that one object can have several names.

At a slightly later stage, naming systems can be discussed; these, in turn, reveal cultural differences. For example, certain Asian cultures have more precise categories than those reflected in the English language for family relationships. Names for relatives on the father's side are different from those in the same physical relationship on the mother's side. Such differences may reflect particular notions of degree or status.

Older children, too, often have the ability to discuss translation choices. This has occurred, in my experience, particularly when translating songs and stories.

(E) Children are aware of different types of discourse

They can indicate that language used for different purposes, in different contexts, or in a different genre, changes in significant ways.

Thus Vicki, again, asked if his group could retell their story like BBC's *Question Time*, began:

> Question Time. This is Question Time. Here is your host, Vicki Sohal. Today we have big Mrs Smith, Jaswinder Bains, Mandeep Devi, Reena Devi. Today we are going to talk about Noah's Ark. We are going to begin the story off, with starting with Miss Devi. Start off, Miss Devi.

He clearly understands the role of chairperson and even achieves the kind of peremptory style associated with certain well-known television interviewers. He knows something of the needs of his viewers and has a sense of structure and sequence.

Hanfia reveals a different sense of genre. When her group of seven-year-olds were trying to describe a large poster, the description emerged as a narrated list:

> I can see a grandmother holding a lollipop with this twig and I can see a boy bursting a balloon with a needle. I can see a grandad eating a cake. The father is taking a picture. The dog is eating the cake.

However, this changed when they were asked to tell a story about the picture. This time Hanfia says:

> One day it was Baljit's birthday and when people came to his party the dog came too. But when Baljit dropped his cake the dog ate it. Mother said she'd give him some other cake. But Baljit could not stop crying because he wanted his own cake.

The story clearly uses different conventions. It has an opening formula ('One day') which sets the scene. It employs a variety of cohesive elements to point forward ('when', 'but', 'because'). It includes a series of characters, with several motives. It demonstrates a significant relationship between cause and effect. In short, it is remarkably different, in content, structure and style, from the earlier list.

(F) Children develop their skills by being used as interpreters

In explaining an activity for another child or adult in mother tongue an interpreter's own learning can be reinforced and a greater understanding revealed than was apparent from observation of their use of English. Here is Asha, 6, explaining Snakes and Ladders in Punjabi to Rajon:

> Yours that way, mine this way. First it's his turn, then it's your turn. Rajon, if it's five you're going to put it on the five. If it's six, put it on the six. It's your go. Which one do you want? When it's your turn, whatever number comes up, put it there.

Finally, there is the whole issue of hidden messages. The act of translating gives children power. In this role children can deduce the intentions of the teacher and adopt part of her role. They can interpret not only the word, but the whole situation.

For example, when in a news session, Harpal said in Punjabi, 'Manjit took me on the bus to get some bananas', Archna translated this into English as a mini-narrative:

He said he went to the shop. He wanted to buy some bananas and he went on a bus to get them from the shop.

When asked another question, Harpal nodded his head. His non-verbal response was 'translated' as:

He said he went to buy something else.

Similarly, as a further example of the exercise of power, children introduce other messages, when they believe that the teacher doesn't understand what is being said. Thus, they might tell some unfortunate child that they must do things properly; that the teacher has forbidden them to go to the toilet; or, when trying to borrow something, 'If you don't give it, you'll have to go out of the class'.

The fact that such manipulation is carried out in a different language from English gives another dimension to the term, 'hidden curriculum', a concept examined in detail in Chapter 6, 'Children as interpreters'.

Monitoring spoken English language development in the early stages

Christine Turner

All children bring to school their own experience of the world. Those children who begin their schooling overseas and then arrive here between the ages of, say, seven and nine years, have to adapt to a new country, a different education system, and an unfamiliar language. Most are old enough to be aware that:

- they have left close relatives and friends behind;
- life in a terraced house in an English city is very different from their previous home in India, Pakistan or Bangladesh (or Vietnam etc.);
- the norms and teaching styles they encounter may be at variance with what they were used to at home;
- their reference points against which to measure experience are confusing;
- they cannot function in a language which, clearly, many younger children have mastered.

Such apparent and temporary deficiencies must be set against positive attributes such as:

- greater knowledge of first language;
- more advanced cognitive development (than a younger child in the same position);
- greater skill to transfer to learning a second language;
- more motivation, perhaps.

This Appendix is about three children who may be considered 'late arrivals'. They are Abdul, Fatima and Yasmina.

ABDUL

Aged 8½
Two years' schooling in Pakistan

Class in England: Year 3
Has two younger sisters at school and a new baby brother
Father has lived in England for many years and speaks English quite well
Mother has been in England ten months and speaks no English
The family speaks Urdu and Punjabi

Abdul is helped in class by Ashraf, who keeps him informed about what is happening and passes on his requests and responses. Whenever Ashraf misses a half-day (which he does frequently), Abdul is rather lost; in the early stages, he often cried. A little later, his most frequent and confident utterance became 'I can't', even at times when he could, in fact, do the task required of him.

Gradually, he began to make progress in various areas, e.g. talking more; trying harder with maths; offering to help; paying more attention in class. He regressed, not surprisingly, when his father went into hospital for an operation. However, after his father's recovery and, more particularly, when a weaker child (Fatima) joined the class, Abdul became quite superior and disparagingly pointed out what she could not do. Only for a while, however; for she caught up fast and this encouraged him to do better.

At the time of writing, his general progress has been fairly good. He has mastered most of the sounds of the letters of the alphabet and is trying hard with reading. He can have an informative, interesting conversation, giving his opinion as needed, with an adult or with other children in a small group, but is still somewhat overwhelmed in the whole-class situation.

Table 1 Observation of language use: Abdul. (*See* Tough 1979)

Child's name: Abdul. Year 3. d.o.b............................ Month of observation:	Nov.	Dec.	Jan.	March	May
Talk with children who use first language:					
Withdrawn or ignoring	✓				
Aware but not participating		✓			
Initiating using L1			✓	✓	✓
Co-operating using L1		✓	✓	✓	✓
Discussing using L1				✓	✓
Directing using L1				✓	✓
Being directed using L1		✓	✓	✓	✓
Talk with adult in L1:					
Reluctant			✓	✓	

Table 1 (continued)

Month of observation:	Nov.	Dec.	Jan.	March	May
Initiates			✓		
Responds when approached			✓	✓	✓
Maintains dialogue with ease				✓	✓
Approach to children who do not speak L1:					
Uses gesture / facial expression			✓		
Uses actions / demonstrates			✓		
Co-operates in activity through non-verbal communication			✓		
Imitates word or phrase in English used by other children					
Co-operates in activity using some English words/phrases					✓
Talk with teacher or adult who does not speak L1:					
Listens when spoken to in English	✓	✓	✓	✓	
Response shows some understanding	✓	✓	✓	✓	
Repeats English word/phrase offered			✓	✓	
Attracts attention with gesture or action			✓	✓	
Initiates with English word/phrase			✓	✓	✓
Responds with English word/phrase	✓	✓	✓	✓	
Self-correction of English			✓	✓	

FATIMA

> Aged 8
> Two years' schooling in Pakistan
> Class in England: Year 3
> Has an older sister, an older brother and a younger sister
> Whole family has been in England seven months
> Father speaks good English
> Mother attends English for Beginners classes
> The family speak Urdu and Punjabi

On admittance to school, Fatima did not know any English. She was very quiet when at her group table and observed everyone and everything with great interest. When talking to her teacher she chattered away in Urdu/Punjabi, not seeming to realize her teacher's incomprehension. She would run about everywhere and throw her arms around her teacher, bubbling over with the newness of everything.

She soon learned to answer her name when the register was being called and, at the beginning of any activity, would watch intently and then begin to do the same, if she was able to.

At the time of writing, Fatima is so determined to learn, to do things, to make things, that she applies herself with great zeal and concentration. She talks non-stop in Urdu/Punjabi, but is adding more and more English all the time. In a group, using an inter-language of Urdu/Punjabi/English, she will ask and answer questions and say what she thinks.

She has learned to form the letters of the English alphabet from scratch. She has also mastered the sounds of most of the letters and can make a

Table 2 Observation of language use: Fatima

Child's name: Fatima. Year 3. d.o.b ....
Month of observation:
Activity: general class routine

	Jan.	Feb.	March	April	May
Talk with children who use first language:					
Withdrawn or ignoring					
Aware but not participating	✓				
Initiating using L1		✓	✓	✓	✓
Co-operating using L1		✓	✓	✓	✓
Discussing using L1		✓	✓	✓	✓
Directing using L1				✓	✓
Being directed using L1	✓	✓	✓	✓	✓
Talk with adult in L1:					
Reluctant					
Initiates	✓	✓	✓	✓	✓
Responds when approached	✓	✓	✓	✓	✓
Maintains dialogue with ease		✓	✓	✓	✓
Approach to children who do not speak L1:					
Uses gesture / facial expression		✓	✓	✓	✓
Uses actions / demonstrates		✓	✓	✓	✓
Co-operates in activity through non-verbal communication			✓	✓	✓
Imitates word or phrase in English used by other children			✓	✓	✓
Co-operates in activity using some English words/phrases				✓	✓
Talk with teacher or adult who does not speak L1:					
Listens when spoken to in English	✓	✓	✓	✓	✓
Response shows some understanding					
Repeats English word/phrase offered	✓	✓	✓	✓	✓
Attracts attention with gesture or action	✓	✓	✓	✓	✓

Table 2   (continued)

Month of observation:	Jan.	Feb.	March	April	May
Initiates with English word/phrase	✓	✓	✓	✓	
Responds with English word/phrase	✓	✓	✓	✓	
Self-correction of English	✓	✓	✓	✓	

good attempt at reading words from the early stages of the reading scheme, 'Link-Up'.

In short, Fatima appears to have adapted extremely well to school, in a very brief period of time.

YASMINA

Fatima's sister, aged almost 9
Four years' schooling in Pakistan
Class in England: Year 4

On admittance to school, Yasmina could answer when she was asked her name in English, could say, and write, English numbers up to 40 (probably more) and could write her name. She gave the impression of being quite mature. Special helpers were assigned to interpret for Yasmina. She appeared to be well received by the class and even the boys explained tasks for her in Urdu/Punjabi.

At the time of writing, Yasmina takes tremendous delight in everything

Table 3 Observation of language use: Yasmina

Child's name: Yasmina. Year 4. d.o.b............................. Month of observation:	Jan	Feb.	March	April	May
Talk with children who use first language:					
Withdrawn or ignoring					
Aware but not participating	✓				
Initiating using L1		✓	✓	✓	✓
Co-operating using L1	✓	✓	✓	✓	✓
Discussing using L1		✓	✓	✓	✓
Directing using L1			✓	✓	✓
Being directed using L1	✓	✓	✓	✓	✓
Talk with adult in L1:					
Reluctant					
Initiates		✓	✓	✓	✓
Responds when approached	✓	✓	✓	✓	✓

Table 3 (continued)

Month of observation:	Jan.	Feb.	March	April	May

Maintains dialogue with ease .... ✓ ...... ✓

Approach to children who do not speak L1:
Uses gesture facial expression .... ✓ ...... ✓ ...... ✓ ...... ✓ ...... ✓
Uses actions / demonstrates .... ✓ ...... ✓ ...... ✓ ...... ✓ ...... ✓
Co-operates in activity through non-verbal
    communication .... ✓ ...... ✓ ...... ✓ ...... ✓ ...... ✓
Imitates word or phrase in English used by other
    children .... ✓ ...... ✓ ...... ✓ ...... ✓
Co-operates in activity using some English
    words/phrases .... ✓ ...... ✓

Talk with teacher or adult who does not speak L1:
Listens when spoken to in English .... ✓ ...... ✓ ...... ✓ ...... ✓ ...... ✓
Response shows some understanding .... ✓ ...... ✓ ...... ✓
Repeats English word/phrase offered .... ✓ ...... ✓ ...... ✓
Attracts attention with gesture or action .... ✓
Initiates with English word/phrase .... ✓
Responds with English word/phrase .... ✓ ...... ✓ ...... ✓
Self-correction of English .... ✓ ...... ✓ ...... ✓ ...... ✓

Table 4 National Curriculum Attainment Targets (ATs)

	Abdul (after 7 months in school)	Fatima (5 months in school)	Yasmina (5 months in school)
AT 1: Speaking & Listening	Level 3	Level 1	part Level 2
AT 2: Reading	Level 1 + begin. Lev. 2	Level 1	Level 2
AT 3: Writing	Level 1 + begin. Lev. 2	Level 1	Level 1 + begin. Lev. 2
AT 4: Spelling	Level 2	Level 1	Level 2
AT 5: Handwriting	Level 2	Level 2	Level 2 + Level 3

she does and when she masters something (for example, a new word such as a colour, or a phrase such as, 'Please give me the scissors'), she always wants to use it and ask if it is right. She loves words, always asks to take home writing to copy, and is pleased that her mother is learning English.

Although still rather diffident about speaking in front of her class, Yasmina will choose her moment to speak to her teacher (in English). She seems to want to be certain that something is correct before she says it. When necessary, she will use Urdu/Punjabi without embarrassment.

Yasmina has settled into school routine pretty well, considering how short a time she has been in England. On the whole, she is happy in school, though she says that, at times, she misses her friends in Pakistan. Her achievements with English and other curriculum areas have been considerable, and she shows great promise for her future.

ACQUIRING A SECOND LANGUAGE: FAVOURABLE CONDITIONS

- sympathetic, warm, secure environment (with adults, peers)
- sensitivity to child's linguistic and cultural background
- encouragement from: parents/classmates/teachers/others
- use of L1 to express needs, queries, fears, interests
- opportunities to relax and chat in L1
- promotion of L1 to support new learning
- use of a classmate as interpreter
- encouragement of gestures and facial expressions
- repetition of essential words and structures
- practical activities to ensure involvement
- opportunities to participate in group work:
  (a) in the classroom
  (b) in a quieter, less distracting setting
- child's own motivation, interests, expectations, support.

Monitoring spoken English language development through four stages

Jean Mills

No spoken language checklist is perfect, but all have the potential to sharpen our awareness and, occasionally, to remind us of what we might otherwise overlook. The checklist now offered for scrutiny (which took as its starting-point the levels proposed by Hilary Hester 1990) is divided into four stages:

Stage 1: for children new to learning English;
Stage 2: for those becoming acquainted with the language;
Stage 3: for those becoming confident as users of English;
Stage 4: for experienced and near fluent users.

The checklist is further divided into three areas, viz. those indicating:

* social and/or linguistic competence;
* language functions or purposes;
* command of vocabulary or syntax.

These three areas will, inevitably, overlap at some points, but are deliberately kept separate here in order to highlight different aspects of the language learning process. Some parts of the checklist may be completed by ticks (as in the earlier checklist in Appendix 3). Other parts require the recording of particular words or phrases. In this respect, the stress falls on listening carefully to what the children actually say, and forming judgements about those utterances.

Table 5 Language development checklist: Stage 1

Social/linguistic competence

* observes carefully what others are
  doing and imitates them ....

Table 5 (continued)

- makes verbal (L1/L2) contact
  with another pupil in class ....

- joins in activities ....

- uses L1 in some class activities ....

- uses body language to communicate ....

- approaches adult to make needs known ....

- follows a one-part simple
  instruction (e.g. 'Put it in the bin') ....

- uses context clues to
  understand simple instructions ....

Language functions/purposes

- evidence of use of different language
  functions in L1, e.g.

  (a) telling a story; ....

  (b) holding a conversation; ....

  (c) exploring a problem ....

Vocabulary/syntax

- uses single words (e.g. 'toilet') ....

- uses two-word combinations
  (e.g. 'I finished') ....

- imitates short phrases (e.g. 'Can you
  help me?') ....

- names personal possessions ....

- names classroom objects..

- vocabulary of immediate family
  (daddy, mummy, sister, brother) ....

- uses complete phrases (e.g. 'my
  sister glove', 'baby walking') ....

Table 6 Language development checklist: Stage 2

Social/linguistic competence

- strives to communicate regardless of correctness ....

- joins in activities using English ....

- initiates conversations with peers ....

- directs actions of others ....

- evidence of understanding more English than can use ....

Language functions/purposes

- understands simple stories and can retell a shortened version in English, with support ....

- takes/brings a simple oral message in English ....

- gives short report of a personal event, using simple tenses ....

Vocabulary/syntax

- developing vocabulary (e.g. body parts, everyday objects, relations); more extensive classroom vocabulary ....

- can put objects into simple categories (e.g. animals, food, vehicles) ....

- asks simple questions (e.g. 'Where?' 'Can I?') ....

- uses some pronouns increasingly appropriately (e.g. he/she;him/her) ....

- uses some adjectives (e.g. colour, size, quantity) ....

- uses simple adverbs (e.g. quickly, slowly) ....

- combines/expands simple phrases (e.g. 'my baby this big', 'him floor falling', water jumping up ground') ....

Table 7 Language development checklist: Stage 3

Social/linguistic competence

- uses English confidently but still some inaccuracies (e.g. 'I gone', 'It will get break')...

- requires support in subject areas ....

- interacts confidently with peers and adults...

- contributes to large-group discussions ....

Language functions/purposes

- can carry out simple role plays (e.g. family situations, school) ....

- can give a simple description (e.g. of picture, object, person)...

- can sequence events using simple connectives (e.g. 'then', 'and', 'but')................................

- can give reasons ('If','because' ,'might') and predict events ....

- can make comparisons ('bigger', 'longer', 'hotter')...

Vocabulary/syntax

- English shows some features of L1 (e.g. pronunciation, lack of articles)................................

- increasing vocabulary to extended environment (e.g. can identify most objects in reading book; weather, seasons, animals)...

- pronunciation generally accurate (but 'arxed?' 'crips?' 'sockses?')..

- paraphrases/substitutes when English vocabulary unknown (e.g. 'he putting flower', i.e. 'watering')...

- increasing use of prepositions (e.g. 'behind', 'in front of', 'between', 'over', 'through')...

Table 7 (continued)

- uses question words (e.g. 'who?'
  'when?' 'how?' 'whose?')...

- greater range of tenses: future
  ('will'; past 'have'/'had';
  past continuous 'was going')..

Table 8 Language development checklist: Stage 4

Social/linguistic competence

- uses English with confidence
  in most social situations ....

- requires support in some subject
  areas with specialized vocabulary (e.g.
  Science; History)..

- interacts confidently in group
  discussions ....

- moves easily between L1 and L2 ....

- gaps in understanding
  extended monologue..

- gaps in detail when
  hearing unfamiliar accents...

- asks for clarification
  (e.g. 'What do you call it?')..

Language functions/purposes

- can retell a story at length ....

- can describe accurately...

- can explain a process ....

- can switch between functions
  with little difficulty, within
  the same oral comment..

Table 8 Continued

Vocabulary/syntax

- uses many tenses appropriately...

- uses greater variety of
  connectives (e.g. 'first', 'after', 'when')...

- uses some complex question
  structures (e.g. 'Could you?'
  'Do you?' 'Would you?') ....

Chapter 4

Assessing in mother tongue
Sukhwant Kaur and Richard Mills

EDITORS' INTRODUCTION

We now move on to the area of testing individual children through their mother tongue. This chapter follows a case-study approach to two children, Punjabi-speakers, newly arrived from India. As the account makes clear, a lot of information was collected about the children from a variety of contexts. This information included responses when they were tested on certain maths concepts using Punjabi.

The process raised several areas of concern, particularly:

- the effects that translation has on test items;
- the interpretation of responses to test items;
- the cultural bias revealed, even in such an apparently straightforward area as mathematics.

Such concerns have by no means been addressed in present arrangements for Standard Assessment Tasks (SATs); and, indeed, discussion of such issues appears embryonic, since it often relies on broad assumptions rather than detailed evidence, of the kind presented here.

What this analysis suggests is that, certainly, mother-tongue assessment is a valid undertaking, but that the circumstances in which it is carried out need to be clarified if it is to be fair to the children involved. Thus, a SAT-type test should be yet one more aspect of an assessment that has already taken into account the child's previous learning experiences and the concepts developed both in English and in mother tongue.

At best, bearing in mind the limitations outlined in the chapter, such assessments provide additional information. At worst, given the level of resourcing required and the concomitant demands on all involved, they could proceed as a crude, piecemeal approach, baffling to both children and teachers.

I say, 'Weigh them for me.' Then, when I watch him, I'll say, 'You've done that wrong. I'll hand you over to the police.' He'll say, 'No, don't give me over to the police.'

(eight-year-old girl, in Punjabi)

At one time, non-English-speakers in school were felt to be problem children. Perhaps this is still the case in some areas, but the pendulum has clearly swung in their favour. They are now regarded by many in a positive light as speakers of other languages, rather than non-speakers of English. Such a shift of perspective, amounting to a sea-change in attitude, presents the children as language and cultural resources in their own right, to be drawn on for the benefit of the whole school community, and not merely for children from ethnic minority groups, as Tansley's survey (1986) indicates has been the case.

In keeping with this positive image, an early TGAT (Task Group on Assessment and Testing) document, prefiguring National Curriculum assessment, acknowledged the special position of bilingual and developing bilingual children by informing teachers that assessment 'should, wherever practicable and necessary, be conducted in the pupil's first language' (1987).

This intriguing statement, tentative as it was, masked the many problems inherent in attempting to assess through mother tongue. It was, and is, a worthy enough intention, but its implementation, in any academically respectable way, is far from straightforward, as will be shown.

Following the establishment of the National Curriculum, material was gathered from observing two Punjabi-speaking children. They were newly arrived in England from India: Mandeep, aged eight, and her brother, Kuldip, aged six. When first encountered, they had been attending an inner-city primary school for some seven months. Mandeep had attended school in India for three years and Kuldip for three months.

Although the children had been observed in many different situations, it was decided to assess them through Punjabi in terms of National Curriculum mathematics because this was felt to be the least ambiguous of all school subjects. Indeed, the Cockcroft Report refers to mathematics as 'a means of communication which is powerful, concise and unambiguous' (1982).

The assessment carried out did reveal many aspects of the children's mathematical knowledge but, ultimately, this was not so important as the insights gained into, and from, the process of mother-tongue testing. It is these that are emphasized in this chapter, rather than the maths results achieved by the children. (Brief details of the tests used are given in Appendix 5.)

Above all, it was discovered that devising, then translating, test items was not so straightforward as might be thought. There were the following difficulties:

(a) Time: the whole process was far more time-consuming than designing a monolingual assessment
(b) Translation problems:
    1   Precise translations were not necessarily accurate translations
    2   Equivalent lexical items, including technical terms, might be lacking or not known
    3   Slight changes of emphasis, including choice of vocabulary, could distort understanding
(c) Recording issues: namely, the use of phonetic script
(d) Cultural bias
(e) National Curriculum assessment limitations

(a) TIME

Now that SATs are in place, will they be available in English only, or in any of the hundred and fifty languages currently spoken somewhere in England? If unavailable in those languages (and how many teachers would be able to read them anyway?), could/should they be translated by individual teachers for individual children? Experience showed the time involved on merely one set of tests to be considerable.

Our tests were devised, first in English and then in Punjabi, over several hours, in collaboration with the school's language support teacher. They were based on Maths Attainment Targets 2, 4 and 8.

Once the assessment had been devised and administered, there was the considerable task of deciphering the children's tape-recorded Punjabi responses and translating them into English, so that they could be noted down and evaluated – a very time-consuming process, particularly as young children's speech is often difficult to determine on audio tape.

(b) TRANSLATION PROBLEMS

In the case of Attainment Target 4: Number, Level 1, the child was asked: 'Without counting, how many... do you think there are?' In Punjabi this strictly and phonetically translates as, 'Ginun dtho bugair dhirah ki kiyal heh bi kineh... heh?' However, saying, 'Ginun dtho bugair, das kineh... heh,? which means, 'Without counting, say how many there are?' is not so accurate a translation, but is far more precise. Hence, in the interests of maintaining a consistently accurate translation, it is difficult to know when to deviate from the exact English form. The process of translation inevitably involves language discrepancies, with concomitant problems when moderating the results.

When it came to devising an assessment which required the children to order a number of objects according to length, a difficulty occurred. The children were asked to order a number of pencils in ascending order of length, because children are generally accustomed to starting with the smallest unit and working up to the biggest. This meant putting the shortest pencil in front of the child first and asking, 'Which is the next longest?' Yet in Punjabi the only way to express this was to say, 'After this one, which is longer?' However, as can be seen in this question, there is no Punjabi equivalent to the sequential lexical item 'next', and because of the wording of the question, the child might have given a pencil that was longer than the one in front of him/her, but not necessarily the next longest. Also, in Punjabi the words for 'long' and 'short' alter according to the gender of the item to which they refer and this is a complication that does not exist in English.

Before assessing it was also necessary to establish whether the children were accustomed to using English numbers and numerals, in case this might cause confusion. Indeed, both *Mathematics 5 to 11* (1979: 15) and the Cockcroft Report (1982: 65/66, paras 221–4) suggest that teachers should take it upon themselves to become acquainted with the number systems that speakers of other languages may be accustomed to. Mandeep, in fact, when asked in English to write the numbers 1 to 10 did so correctly. When asked in Punjabi, she again used English numerals. (See Appendix 6.)

Looking through the Mathematics Attainment Targets, it was evident that we did not know the Punjabi for 'a square, circle, triangle, rectangle, three-dimensional shapes, angles, addition, subtraction or multiplication'. Nor did we know the Punjabi for 'odd' and 'even', as applicable to numbers. Moreover, having made some investigations, it was difficult to be certain at what ages young children in India could be expected to have acquired these concepts anyway.

As may be imagined, in any translation the alteration of merely a few words, or the word order, or the inclusion of an extra word, or the exclusion of merely one word, can totally change the desired emphasis of the phrase or sentence. The meanings, nuances, associations of an item can be changed beyond recognition. Consequently, in the process of translation, clues can either be added, where not desired, or omitted, where necessary. Indeed, the word order can drastically affect which information has most impact and is, therefore, retained in the child's understanding and memory. This raises the question of which should come first, the English or the Punjabi? If assessment is carried out by devising items in English and then translating them, the kind of distortion mentioned above is bound to occur. Perhaps what should happen is that the concept is isolated first and then a question is devised in Punjabi which will assess that concept.

We were struck by other linguistic difficulties. For instance, in Punjabi there is no use of the definite article and there is infrequent use of the subject. Instead, the language is very dependent upon demonstrative pronouns and explanation that is heavily context-related. Punjabi does not seem to be used in the same disembedded, abstract way which is a feature of English, and such differences need to be remembered when analysing children's development in language.

For example, in conversation with Kuldip, he constantly used the demonstrative pronouns to explain his meaning. So, when asked how he made a dung cake, he replied (in Punjabi):

> *This is the choulah* (cooking fire). *You put the dung cake in here. Then you make the vegetable curry.*

Again, when describing a chicken's egg hatching, he said:

> *Like this above. Like this below. It breaks and then the babies come of it.*

Such examples are not conclusive but they are pointers to a difference of approach brought about by one language. How much more variation might be observed in speakers of languages other than Punjabi.

Furthermore, when translating Punjabi into English, there are often several possible English equivalents to choose from. However, although all may convey the same meaning, each one might involve different types of verbs. Thus, in making choices of English equivalents, the interpreter can, inadvertently, make the child's language ability appear more or less advanced than it actually is.

Here, for instance, is an 'accurate' translation of part of a conversation with Kuldip, but it would be unwise to make too many assumptions from it about his linguistic ability. Certainly, he shows himself to be a lively conversationalist, who relates well to his adult partner, requiring only a little prompting. However, the final sentence ('Just as there are ...') shows a structural competence and precision in English which might not be present in the original Punjabi.

SK: *When you wake up in the morning, what do you do first?*
K: *In India, you don't even have toothbrushes.*
SK: *Don't you have toothbrushes? What do you do then?*
K: *You just wash your face and do 'choulie' (gargle).*
SK: *What's that? How do you do it?*

K:	*Then your teeth are alright.*
SK:	*But what is this 'choulie'? I don't know. Explain it to me.*
K:	*You do it like this.* (K demonstrates.)
SK:	*But what do you do it with?*
K:	*With water. You do 'choulie' with water.*
SK:	*Just water! But what do you scrub your teeth with?*
K:	*Your teeth? There aren't brushes there.*
SK:	*What do you use then?*
K:	*There's only that.*
SK:	*What?*
K:	*That to put on your teeth.*
SK:	*What do you call it? Is it called 'dthardthan'?*
K:	*Yes.*
SK:	*Where do you get 'dthardthan' from?*
K:	*Dthardthan. The one that has prickles on it.*
SK:	*Which thing has prickles on it?*
K:	*When the prickles fall off, then you do dthardthan.*
SK:	*What do they fall from?*
K:	*Like this. You pull them off and throw them down from the tree. Just as there are a few trees here, there's the same amount over there.*

The extract is, of course, in line with that 'tradition' of teacher–pupil interrogation, where the teacher (SK) asks the questions on the basis of a combination of assumed and genuine ignorance. But, if we are to be wary of assuming too much from the linguistic structures (as in that last contribution), what we can affirm is Kuldip's ability to signal a direction in the conversation (as in his first comment); to offer additional detail (as in his last three comments) and to respond directly when challenged (throughout). The issue of cultural dissonance will be addressed shortly.

(c) RECORDING ISSUES

None of us involved in these investigations, neither children nor teachers, were literate in Punjabi. This meant that, for the purposes of developing a record, the children's spoken Punjabi needed to be represented phonetically in English. The dangers in such a process are obvious and include strong possibilities of misunderstanding through misinterpretation; distortion by accent; inability to give the benefit of any doubt (as would be done if the transcribing were of an English text). Imagine, too, the problems which such transliteration might pose for any moderator called in to check the script and the assessment based on that script.

If simply translating two basic areas of mathematics assessment into Punjabi involves so many discrepancies, ambiguities and hours of time, then it must be realized that the problem of translating tests in areas which are not always as patterned and logical as mathematics and in which the exact emphasis or individual meaning of a key word is of immense importance, will be proportionally greater.

(d) CULTURAL BIAS

The experience of translating tests aimed at assessing children's abilities to achieve certain attainment targets, and of working with the children on those tests, revealed a cultural bias which was inescapable. This was particularly evident in our work on standardized measurements.

Kuldip and Mandeep had never been to a shop alone and had lived their early years in a society where food products were not sold in metrically accurate quantities in packages clearly labelled with exact amounts. Instead, they had experienced a flexible approach, with customer and shopkeeper matching their wits against each other. Here, for example, Mandeep explains how she and her mother bought mangoes in India.

It was fascinating to note that Mandeep appeared more concerned about the social and cultural aspects of the transaction, about the tactics of buying and outwitting the shopkeeper, than about the units of weight.

M: *If they're big you say 'I want one and a half.' You usually get about four. I go with my mum, but sometimes thieves steal them so you have to carry them carefully. You get on a bus and go. There's no fare for me, one rupee fare for mummy. When you go home, you go on a tampoo* (motorized rickshaw).

SK: *But if you're buying mangoes and you don't just want one or two or three, but want them in terms of weight, how do you ask for some?*

M: *You say, 'Weigh me some.'*

SK: *But how many should he weigh for you?*

M: *He should put one and a half and about five on the other side* (starts to explain what scales look like and how you weigh). *I say, 'Weigh them for me.' Then when I watch him, I'll say, 'You've done that wrong. I'll hand you over to the police.' He'll say, 'No, don't give me over to the police.'*

Mandeep was asked to imagine she was going shopping for her mum. What would she say to the mango seller? She began to imitate the call of the fruit seller:

M:	*'Excuse me Sir, I need some mangoes.' First I ask him how much they are.*
SK:	*And what does he say?*
M:	*If you want four, two rupees, if you want three, one rupee.'*
SK:	*Doesn't he tell you the weight?*
M:	*Not weight, you just ask how much money they ask.*

When we discussed clothing material there was a little more common ground. Here is the exchange when Mandeep was asked how much material she would need to make an Indian suit:

M:	*You say, 'Give me four, five metres.'*
SK:	*So you buy material in metres? What do you buy mangoes in?*
M:	*But that's food and this is material.*
SK:	*If you were buying milk, how much would you ask for?*
M:	*If you want one glass, you say, 'Fill the glass up', and pay one rupee. If you want deaed, they say 'Five'.*
SK:	*If you were buying gold, how much would you ask for?*
M:	*I know this one. You say, 'I want some bangles. Tell us how much money you want. If it's expensive we won't buy.'*
SK:	*How much did they weigh?*
M:	*Not weight. You just ask how much money they ask.*

Many young children, of course, and not merely those brought up in India, would have had difficulty with some of these questions. The exchange was by way of initial skirmish to try to establish some starting-points.

One further item of cross-cultural impact is intriguing. When shown a watch, Mandeep was able to tell that it said one o'clock. However, when asked how long it took for the big hand to go all the way round, she answered, 'Fifty hours'. Now, in certain Punjabi families the answer 'Fifty hours' is given when one wants to register something as taking a very long time. It is not a measurement but more of a subjective comment, rather as in the English saying, 'We walked for miles and miles' (i.e. a long way).

The problem of cultural bias in testing is not, of course, new, but what now gives the debate added impetus is the existence of a National Curriculum. The fear is that the stress on national uniformity may undermine individuality and fail to recognize the strengths of bilingual children. Bourne (1989: 199) comments, 'People in power seem to have some idea of a culturally neutral curriculum... The idea of giving all pupils one "diet", but a diet designed by and for one cultural group... may be inclusive, but is indifferent to diversity, and has in the past appeared to lead to social stratification along socio-economic class and ethnic group lines.'

Assessments cannot emerge out of a vacuum; they inevitably arise from particular contexts. Unless maths test items are entirely computational, they must have some relevance to a recognizable world. However, while 'test constructors have an obligation to ensure that their instruments contain no sexual or racial stereotypes, or any material which could be offensive to a particular group' (TGAT 1987:4.3), those same test constructors, following National Curriculum requirements, will be hard pressed to devise items which are fair to all children, particularly those brought up in certain rural rather than urban environments.

In such areas in some parts of the world, education will be neither compulsory, nor free, nor child-centred. My experience is that, for example, in the Indian Punjab, although nursery education is free, most children only attend school in the primary years which cater for 7 to 11-year-olds. Although tuition is free, the strain of buying all the necessary books and materials puts a heavy, often financially crippling, burden on parents. From the age of eleven onwards all fees, including those for tuition, have to be paid for by parents. With large classes and inadequate resources, practical demonstrations and experiences are not possible. Learning is, therefore, blackboard-based and largely theoretical, and rote learning is the chief method of teaching. The entire class are usually taught at the same pace and are given the same task unless specific severe learning difficulties are evident.

In the primary years, the teaching of addition, division and multiplication is the main core of children's mathematical learning. The idea of discovery learning, and learning through play, is not a part of Punjabi educational thinking. Three-dimensional shapes, angles, volume and capacity are certainly not part of primary education, although some oral teaching of weight equivalents may take place. So the content of National Curriculum tests would not be directly applicable to children who have been taught in a different context. This leads to the question of whether assessment which aims to determine if children are sufficiently equipped to cope with life in one country, can fairly be applied to children who have received their education in another.

(e) NATIONAL CURRICULUM ASSESSMENT LIMITATIONS

The initial assessment, according to National Curriculum criteria, of children recently arrived from overseas, can take little, if any, account, either of the education received in the home country, or of the speed at which new learning has been assimilated. The latter could only be addressed in later assessment, after National Curriculum work had been followed for a defined period. For this reason, concepts of ability, experiential knowledge and skills need to be kept discrete and not used inter-changeably.

Bourne (1989) highlights these distinctions when she writes:

> The introduction of standardised assessments in the future may not be helpful in avoiding the conflation of the two quite different concepts of 'ability' and 'English language skills'. Indeed, the presence of bilingual children raises awkward questions about the way 'ability' is both defined and monitored for all pupils. It may be necessary to question critically the whole notion of 'ability' and to work from the position that children come to school with very different experiences, for example, of print, of literacy activities and of child–adult interactions. For while assessments may inform teachers of what children could or could not do in the particular context of the testing situation itself, it will remain up to teachers to work out what sorts of experiences children need in order to develop the concepts required by the education system, and to organise classrooms in order to provide an environment and activities within which such concepts and skills can be developed.

Two examples from Kuldip and Mandeep take these points further.

It became evident that Kuldip did not know the name of the shapes 'square' and 'rectangle' in Punjabi but did know them in English. This illustrates the phenomenon identified by Appel and Muysken (1987) of 'lexical transfer from the second into the first language in the form of loan words'. But, more than this, it reveals how inappropriate it is to test *all* non-English-speakers in Punjabi, when particular children may be able to name certain attributes in one language only. Such an example of 'inter-language strategy' (ibid.) highlights the need for National Curriculum guidelines to clarify the circumstances in which children should be assessed through mother tongue. These will vary from person to person and situation to situation.

On another occasion, Mandeep was busy doing a Winnie the Pooh jigsaw puzzle. When asked what animal it was she answered that it was not an animal but a stuffed toy like the ones you buy in a shop. She said you could sew one, and went on to explain something, but could not make herself understood. She was frustrated by the incomprehension and said, *'How can I explain it?'* She then pulled an acetate sheet out of the scrap box and folded it in half. She said, *'you draw the bear on here and cut it out. You then have two pieces. You put stuffing in the middle and stitch it up to get a soft toy.'*

Such information, obtained through informal discussion, highlights the importance of assessing through mother tongue to determine what children know, but does not necessarily add to the value of assessing the

National Curriculum through mother tongue. Would a National Curriculum test have revealed this information about Mandeep's learning or way of thinking?

As a follow-up, Mandeep was asked which she enjoyed most out of writing and number work. She said number work was her favourite. When asked why she preferred number work, she said, (in Punjabi), *'Number work is important because if two children are asked to hold up ten fingers and one child puts up ten and the other three, when the teacher came to marking it she would need to know which one was right.'* Mandeep appeared to be commenting on the concrete logic inherent in mathematics.

Such examples illustrate the fallibility of a one-off test. Several assessments, over time, in a variety of contexts and in an informal manner, are much more successful in building up a cumulative profile of attainment. Moreover, such insights as those revealed in these mother-tongue situations would be hidden not only from a monolingual teacher but also from a mother-tongue teacher testing restricted items in translation in strict conformity to National Curriculum requirements. In this regard, mother-tongue peripatetics hired to or by school, merely for the purpose of conducting Standard Assessment Tasks, will be limited in the amount and quality of information they may glean.

CONCLUSIONS

The purpose of this chapter has been to show that the simply expressed view that developing bilingual children should experience National Curriculum assessment in mother tongue needs considerable scrutiny.

At one level, the resource and logistical implications seem overwhelming. At a deeper level, translation issues call into question the value of any 'results' which may emerge. Furthermore, the decision as to who might benefit from mother-tongue assessment, in the light of their own previous experience of schooling and teaching in mother tongue, remains problematic.

What should occur is a substantial review, at the highest level, of the resource and training implications of mother-tongue National Curriculum assessment, given the apparent commitment to that concept. What is more likely to occur, one suspects, is an *ad hoc*, piecemeal approach by individual schools and teachers, using mother-tongue testing when and where they can. In other words, doing their best for their children, despite the odds against them.

Appendix 5

Concepts tested

These were as follows:

(a) Attainment Target 2: Number
   Level 1
   Counting objects up to 5. Up to 10. Writing numbers 1 to 10. Ordering
   numbers 1 to 10.
   Level 2
   Writing numbers 1 to 100. Ordering number 1 to 100.
   Recognizing ½s and ¼s.

(b) Attainment Target 4: Number
   Level 1
   Estimation 1 to 10. Estimation 1 to 20.

(c) Attainment Target 8: Number:
   Level 1
   Concepts of 'long' and 'short', 'longer' and 'longest', 'next longest'.
   Level 2
   Using non-standard measurements (i.e. handspans).
   Recognizing the need to use standard units.
   Knowing the most commonly used units of measurement.

Appendix 6

Punjabi numbers

One source of potential confusion between English and Punjabi relates to numbers 1 to 10. In their written form in Punjabi, as Figure 5 shows, some (i.e. 2, 3, 7, 9) have a very close equivalent in English. Others (i.e. 1, 4, 5) have an English equivalent, but not the 'right' one.

For children who know their Punjabi numbers, one imagines that learning the English numbers could be expected to be quite confusing, at least in the early stages.

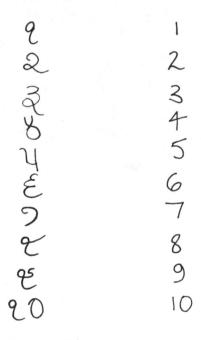

Figure 5   Punjabi numbers

Chapter 5

Assessing in English and mother tongue

Nabela Mann and Richard Mills

EDITORS' INTRODUCTION

In the previous chapter a query was raised concerning the confusion which many teachers feel, when trying to distinguish between children's abilities across curriculum areas and their ability in English language. In some circumstances, it is not easy to say if children have learning difficulties or are unable to show attainment because they have to use English, a language they are still grappling with.

This study focuses on a small group of reception children aged four, some of whom had been designated as slow learners. Their teacher was unsure about this label and felt it would be valuable to compare certain features of their Punjabi and their English, as they responded to particular tasks. How comparable was their achievement in English and in Punjabi?

In general, the results were predictable; in detail, they were not. The findings should, as in the previous chapter, warn us of the pitfalls of making the easy assumption that all children will benefit from being assessed through their mother tongue. Several issues need to be teased out. What is, in fact, a child's mother tongue? How is it related to the language in which children prefer to respond? What of children who switch between languages when trying to convey their meaning? How do teachers indicate the option of such code-switching?

The responses of the children who were surveyed led to a series of home visits. In these, a missing dimension was revealed, namely the extent to which individual parents expressed a strong desire to maintain links with their own cultural roots and their relatives abroad. Such understanding is important for those teachers who wish to appreciate the family aspirations which affect children they teach.

Ayesha attends a local madressa with her older brothers and sisters.

She reads some Urdu and is starting to write it, too. Soon she will begin to learn Arabic, in preparation for the Holy Koran.

(Her mother)

The investigation I am about to describe arose out of concern at the possible underachievement, or perceived underachievement, of certain children in school. The inquiry began in general terms but gradually narrowed its focus as an attempt to discover the proficiency in spoken English and Punjabi of five reception children (aged 5), by testing them practically in the areas of language, mathematics and science.

This experience led from the daytime classroom into the home after school, as I made arrangements to interview the parents of these children. My intention was to learn about the parents' attitudes towards their children's language learning and, at the same time, to discover for myself something of the home context from which the children came and which, inevitably, exercised a great influence upon them.

At the time, I was working in an inner-city primary school with 85 per cent of its children of Asian origin. Most classrooms contained a majority of Muslim children whose first language was the Mirpuri variety of Punjabi, closely followed by Urdu. As an Urdu/Punjabi-speaking Muslim myself, I found it easy to identify with this particular context.

Many of the reception class children had been in school for only two terms, having had no prior experience of nursery education. I initially used English with them, but such was the lack of response that, after a week or so, I began to communicate in mother tongue. The effects were impressive. Interacting with me in their mother tongue seemed to come naturally to many members of the class, especially the girls. The children seemed to put special effort into their work, aware that I could discuss their pictures with them.

A colleague, who noticed how particular children responded positively to me, commented especially on the 'slow learners'. I queried the validity of this term. Were these children indeed 'slow' at learning or had their true understanding been masked by English language difficulty? It was this question which led me to attempt to assess something of their comparative understanding in English and Punjabi. Since the children were unable to write in either language, I chose to carry out, over a 12-month period, a series of practical activities requiring oral responses.

LANGUAGE ACTIVITIES

The group chosen for this scrutiny consisted of three girls – Sofia, Ayesha, Naima – and two boys, Hafeez and Ajit. The girls commonly used their mother tongue when playing and chatting, but rarely in the classroom. The boys generally used English throughout the day.

Each child was given ample opportunity to respond in both languages, as activities were carried out in English first, then Punjabi, and vice versa. The translations were carefully done in order to ensure comparability within each language, although one is aware of the difficulty of achieving this, as is pointed out in Chapter 4. Activities included:

- Issuing classroom instructions. The intention here was to cover the National Curriculum Key Stage 1, Attainment Target 1, Level 1, that children should be able to 'respond appropriately to simple instructions given by a teacher' (e.g. 'Fetch me a pair of scissors' and, rather harder, 'Put the book on the shelf').
- Distinguishing between certain concepts (e.g. hot/cold; before/after; day/night.)
- Requiring children to produce descriptive language (e.g. by asking what was wrong in a particular picture, such as a person ironing with a kettle).
- Seeking logical connection (e.g. by asking children to identify links between two pictures, such as one of children laughing and one of clowns).
- Understanding two simple stories in the same series (i.e. one in English, about Jealous Jim, an ambulance, and one in Punjabi, about Big Billy, a fire-engine).

MATHEMATICS AND SCIENCE ACTIVITIES

These included:

- Estimating (e.g. by asking children to guess the number of cupfuls of sand needed to fill a bucket, before they actually filled it).
- Sorting/ordering/comparing (e.g. by requiring children to recognize various small objects; to sort them into categories of size; to arrange in a series).
- Weighing.
- Discriminating in terms of height and thickness.

Further science activities included:

- Planting seeds (with a stress on the sequence of events and the reasons for each stage in the sequence).
- Floating and sinking.

FINDINGS

Simple tables are given in Appendix 7 which highlight some of the differences in the English/Punjabi understanding of the five children.

Table 9 reveals that all fared significantly better when tested in their mother tongue. This is particularly true for Sofia and Ayesha, where results show that almost a quarter more prepositions were grasped in Punjabi. Table 10 indicates many instances of instructions being misunderstood in English, but much less so in the corresponding Punjabi tests.

Such results could probably have been predicted, given the duration and kind of schooling experienced by these children. However, what is important, I feel, is the amount of detailed information which the assessments revealed about individual children, information denied to a monolingual English-speaking teacher.

For instance, take the case of Naima. She had not been included in the first two tests but was involved in distinguishing between such terms as: 'hot', 'cold'; 'before', 'after'; 'day', 'night'. The results were decisive in revealing her understanding. She had failed to comprehend any of these terms when asked in English or when she was required to supply the appropriate term herself. However, when given the same test in Punjabi, quite the opposite occurred. Not only could she identify the terms, but she also displayed ease when using them in descriptions. Had she not been thus assessed, one might have failed to recognize some of her true capabilities. From that point on, it became impossible to do other than regard Naima in the light of this new understanding about her.

A specific example will serve to illustrate the point. The following answers were given by the girls for two different cards, in answer to the question, 'Can you tell me what's wrong in this card?'

Card 1 showed a woman ironing with a kettle. Responses in English were:

Sofia:	Coffee.
Ayesha:	(Points to kettle, but no oral comment.)
Naima:	Hot ... water.

Card 2 showed a bird flying upside down. Responses in Punjabi were:

Sofia:	*That's wrong. It should be this way* (showing correct position with hand).
Ayesha:	*It's upside down, the bird.*
Naima:	*It's a bird. It's flying wrong way. Wrong way.*

The Punjabi responses show the girls as perfectly capable of identifying the problem and using good descriptive vocabulary to make clear their comprehension of the fault.

A further illumination occurred in analysis of the boys' responses to two pairs of picture cards. Only after Punjabi questioning did Hafeez make clear the link between children laughing (on one card) and a clown (on the other card.) Ajit, on the other hand, discovered that successful communication for him lay in using a combination of English and Punjabi. In response to seeing a card of a boy climbing and one of a boy eating an apple, he said (with Punjabi in italics):

> *Boy* went up. *Climbing tree. Boy* eating apple.
> There's apples.

Thus, the combination of languages enabled Ajit to say all he wanted. It was, I felt, a very positive sign of a child who could creatively manipulate his two languages, an example of 'interlanguage', as defined in *Introduction: Setting the scene*. Noting abilities such as this should be an important consideration in National Curriculum assessment of bilingual children, where one would, presumably, need to determine the extent to which a child knew he/she was using a combination of two languages and could, in fact, differentiate between them.

The pattern was repeated in the story tests of 'Jealous Jim' and 'Big Billy'. The English version elicited little response, whether of words or body language; in fact, one word only from Ayesha, 'crashed'. Not so the Punjabi version of 'Big Billy', where Ayesha says (in Punjabi): '*The fire had gone out and then he started to cry … Billy said, "I didn't put out the fire. It went out itself"'* (imitating the voice of Big Billy).

These were not isolated responses but were mirrored by the other children.

Again, when occupied silently in the ordering of objects from largest to smallest, Sofia failed in English. (Ayesha was successful.) In the Punjabi version, both girls expressed their thought processes aloud, discussing the size of each object in the sequence and comparing it orally with the previous object.

I found this particularly fascinating, as I knew the children had not been taught these concepts in school in mother tongue. Despite that, they could use the more familiar language as a tool for reasoning. When National Curriculum testing started, it was common to hear teachers say: 'It's not fair to test children using mother tongue unless they have been taught these concepts through mother tongue'. My evidence suggests this is not necessarily the case. Rather, it seems that familiarity with language and context has enhanced reasoning power. The children's abilities were more advanced than an assessment in English would have shown.

The findings from Test 4 to do with weight were important as they again showed children performing with greater accuracy and depth in mother tongue than in English (see Tables 13 and 14 in Appendix 7). The same result is seen, in even starker form, in Test 6. Here, the vast difference between children's understanding displayed in both their languages leaps off the page (see Table 15). Only Sofia was able to perform the whole exercise correctly in both English and Punjabi.

The key seems to lie in flexibility. In other words, the children's performance improved when they were able and prepared to move between languages, as they determined, and to employ a combination of the two. Ajit, for instance, understood a task better when it was put to him in Punjabi, but he replied either in English or in a combination of English and Punjabi. Sofia and Ayesha reasoned aloud in Punjabi, even though they had not been taught particular concepts in that language.

Are such findings to be expected? They may be, but one simply does not know, since there are few detailed studies at present. Moreover, testing five children in this way is very different from dealing with twenty-five or even more. The logistics of the task in a school containing 85 per cent developing bilinguals are quite daunting.

This becomes even clearer when one considers the urgent need to learn more about the homes from which our children come. Such discussion of parental aspirations, such knowledge of family history and background, may alter the way we teach, should modify our attitudes, and could even lead to a change in school policy.

Accordingly, I made arrangements to visit the homes of four of the five children. Part of our discussion (in Punjabi or English, as appropriate) was to do with such matters as country of birth; duration of residence in England; languages used in the home; interests and hobbies of the children. The other part related to what I had learnt in the tests about each child. In other words, it was, at best, a mutual exchange of information – and, I believe, valued by the parents as such.

SOFIA'S PARENTS

Sofia's mother spoke in a very strong Punjabi accent, could not read or write in her mother tongue and, as the family had only been together in Britain for three years (arriving from Pakistan, where Sofia had been born), knew no English either. Sofia's father had moved to Britain several years in advance of the rest of the family and spoke some English although he preferred to communicate in Punjabi. Sofia's mother politely declined to answer my questions, preferring to awaken her sleeping husband (a night-shift worker) instead.

He told me that Sofia watched Pakistani video films daily on her return from school, or listened to traditional music on Asian radio stations. No English was spoken in the home and, since the family lived in an area of families of Asian origin, there was no need to speak English in the community.

Sofia's father recognized her weakness in English:

> She cannot speak proper English and we are worried about this. She should be able to speak good English now she's at school.

Not only did his own work make contact difficult but there was a baby to look after. So, in answer to my question about why Sofia could name all the primary colours in English but not in Punjabi, he said:

> Well, I suppose it's because they teach these things at school, but at home we don't. You see I work nights in a factory so I hardly get to see Sofia when she's up and that's why I cannot help her with her English. Sofia's mother does not work except that she sews quite a bit, but she's busy looking after the little one all day. So it doesn't really surprise me that Sofia doesn't know her Punjabi colours.

He was aware, too, that she could not count in either language:

> Sofia still can't count to five. We try telling her, but she keeps forgetting. I don't know. She's just not very clever.

Both parents needed the reassurance that, since Sofia had not been in England as long as some of her peers, she would need more time and experiences with the English language before she could make dramatic progress. Moreover, without media and community imperatives to learn English, and given the home situation, it would have been fruitless and inappropriate to encourage Sofia's parents to cultivate more English at home. They were, in fact, far better placed to develop her Punjabi skills and this they would, no doubt, do.

AYESHA'S MOTHER

Born in Pakistan, and a resident in England for only six years, Ayesha's young mother warmly welcomed the opportunity to talk in Punjabi about the family. She came across to me as a shy, homesick, patriotic person. Her husband (who spoke English) was kept busy all hours as a taxi driver and her time was spent in sewing and in looking after the children, including two still under 3 years old.

She acknowledged the need for her daughter to do well in English but felt that was the school's job. Hers was to maintain cultural identity by giving a solid grounding in Punjabi:

> I hope to return to my home country when the children have finished their education here, and that is why we put great emphasis on our children speaking Punjabi with us in the home.

She was proud that Ayesha was good enough at Punjabi to be able to learn to read and write Urdu at the local madressa and this confirmed my own awareness, in the tests, of her considerable competence in Punjabi. In fact, Ayesha's mother was proud of her on all fronts. She testified:

> Ayesha is a very good girl. She plays happily with her brothers and sisters. There's not much room in the house, especially now with the baby. Nevertheless, Ayesha plays all sorts of games. She likes helping me and watching Pakistani films together.

HAFEEZ'S PARENTS

Hafeez's mother and father are estranged from one another, and not on speaking terms. Mother lives with the children in the family home and father often comes to visit. Both were interested and keen to talk with me but would not sit in the same room together. In fact, their attitude towards the children's language and culture had, according to the father, become a major source of friction between them:

> She cannot see my point of view in this issue or in any other. I try to explain to her, but she thinks I'm trying to be too Westernized. That is why we don't get on. She doesn't understand the need for her children to use English in the home as well as in the school.

Hafeez's father had been away from Pakistan for almost two decades and his experiences had convinced him of the need for his children to become competent users of English. As he said:

> The children speak mostly in English and when we are together I always speak in English with them. I have good reason for this, too. They don't need Punjabi as much as they need to speak and understand English. After all, they are going to spend the rest of their lives here, so I always encourage Hafeez to speak in English.

Hafeez's mother, on the other hand, had a very different view. She held her mother tongue in highest esteem. She felt the need for Hafeez to acquire full competence in Punjabi, not only to assist his understanding of Asian society, but also for communication with other people of Asian origin, especially in the case of a temporary or permanent return to Pakistan. She spoke feelingly about the issue:

> I have not been in this country for many years and it does not mean much to me now that my husband and I do not understand one another. I want my children to grow up respecting their home country and culture, for that's all we have here. I know English is important, too, but when my children are with me I like to hear them speak to me in Punjabi. They can use English any time at school, or when they are playing, and this is good for them. But they must be able to speak fluent Punjabi by the time they grow up so that, when we go to Pakistan to visit, they will be able to understand what their grandparents and relatives are saying to them. That is why I will send Hafeez to a madressa when he is older, so that he can learn to read the Koran and write Urdu, too. That is what I would really like for Hafeez.

AJIT'S MOTHER

Having been born and bred in England, Ajit's mother saw this country, and not India, as her home. However, this did not mean that she accepted English culture as her own. So, while she spoke mostly English at home, she had also taught all her children Punjabi before they were of school age. Hence, Punjabi was Ajit's first language but, as was seen in the testing, his English is not only proficient but also preferred, at least at school. Ajit's mother found this satisfying:

> The children know they can speak in any tongue they wish. They understand Punjabi and I think that is important, even if they can't speak it well. As our children will spend their lives in this country, I see English as the most important language. All the same, we do not overlook our culture or religion (Sikh), which we're very proud of. We educate our children about such matters in Punjabi.

Ajit's mother was not surprised that he knew his colours better in English than Punjabi since English was the language in which she referred to colours:

> You know what it's like when you're talking in Punjabi, with many of the things you say, you automatically use the English word.

This was different with the test concepts of 'thick' and 'thin', which were much more likely to be referred to in Punjabi since 'they probably carry more emphasis' in that language.

As for Ajit himself, he was clearly very active at home, a boy with lively interests. His mother listed some of them:

Colouring, writing, watching TV, playing football. Actually, I've just bought him a cricket set, so he's into that at the moment, thinking he's a little Sunil Gavaskar!

Ajit is always busy doing something.

FINAL NOTE

One cannot generalize from such brief encounters but common threads stand out. Indeed, some of them are threads which I recognize in my own family history.

When my father first moved to Britain in the late 1950s, it was to find employment, but he returned to Pakistan after ten years to marry his 16-year-old bride, later to become my mother. Just like the mothers of Ayesha and Hafeez, she came to England with little education and no knowledge of the language or culture.

The main reason my parents had for bringing up my brother and me in this country was to ensure that we would benefit from the very best education. However, they always hoped to return to Pakistan once we had completed our education. For this reason, we maintained our culture and language. My mother ensured that I spoke fluent Punjabi by the time I went to school. Indeed, like Sofia and Ayesha, initially I was only allowed to speak to my parents in my mother tongue. Later, as they realized the need for instruction in English, so I learnt English. As we lived in an almost entirely 'white' area, I had no difficulty in acquiring my second language.

Now my parents, my brother and I have all settled in our jobs and have no communication complications. In actual fact, my mother has now lived in England longer than all her years spent in Pakistan. With time, the attitudes of my parents have mellowed. I know they would now find it very difficult to return to Pakistan. As for my brother and me, we have two countries, as we have two languages.

Appendix 7

Test results

Table 9 Number of instructions (out of 14) understood

	In English	*In Punjabi*
Sofia	9	13
Ayesha	10	14
Hafeez	12	13
Ajit	11	12

Table 10 Prepositions not understood

	In English	*In Punjabi*	*In both*
Sofia	on; under; in front of		behind
Ayesha	under; in front of behind		
Hafeez	behind		in front of
Ajit	behind	under	in front of

Table 11 Number of 'What's wrong?' cards (out of 4) understood

	In English	*In Punjabi*
Sofia	1	3
Ayesha	0	4
Naima	0	4
Hafeez	3	3
Ajit	2	3

Table 12   Number of 'Why? Because' cards (out of 8) understood

	In English	In Punjabi
Sofia	6	7
Ayesha	4	7
Naima	4	7
Hafeez	5	8
Ajit	4	8

Table 13   Number of correct responses (out of 4) to weight-sorting tasks

	In English	In Punjabi
Sofia	4	4
Ayesha	4	4
Naima	2	1
Hafeez	3	4
Ajit	1	4

Table 14   Number of weight tasks understood (3 comparing and 3 ordering)

	Comparing in English	In Punjabi	Ordering in English	In Punjabi
Sofia	3	3	1	2
Ayesha	1	3	1	3
Naima	1	2	0	3
Hafeez	3	3	3	3
Ajit	2	3	1	3

Table 15   Number of discriminatory terms (out of 6) understood, to do with thickness

	In English	In Punjabi
Sofia	6	6
Ayesha	0	6
Naima	0	6
Hafeez	3	6
Ajit	2	6

Section III

The bilingual experience

Chapter 6

Children as interpreters

Sukhwant Kaur and Richard Mills

EDITORS' INTRODUCTION

Many people in Britain are bilingual. They can speak, and perhaps read, two or more languages. In London, alone, over 150 languages are spoken. So, in theory, there are plenty of people around who can interpret for those who lack the appropriate language. In practice, of course, the match in school, if not at home, may be very difficult. One school has one child only who speaks Lwo; a second school cannot get letters translated into Pashtu; a third school has several potential interpreters among its children, but cannot be sure of the accuracy or appropriateness of their translations.

This chapter addresses the issue of interpretation in considerable depth, with material culled from some fifty-two interviews with children, parents and teachers.

What emerges is that the role of the interpreter is a complex one where matters of relationship, status, sensitivity, power, responsibility, may be as significant as those of knowledge and accuracy. The spotlight within the chapter is not on the role of interpreter within the classroom (that is addressed in Appendix 8), but, rather, on that role within the family and the wider community. What is revealed is a rich pattern of shifting and subtle relationships, with insights about language and personality granted to young interpreters prematurely, by virtue of the maturing situations in which they find themselves.

Teachers often claim to learn much about children by meeting their parents. Many parents of bilingual boys and girls are forced to act through their children. Those children may literally be a lifeline for their parents. As one mother says, 'What is life when you can't speak to anyone?'

This chapter takes us into the world of the interpreter and the interpreted.

When I say, 'Mum, you don't speak English properly', she says, 'Don't complain. You can't speak Punjabi properly.

(Parvinda)

As a bilingual person who started infant education in Britain with Punjabi as my mother tongue, and English as a second language, I have only one recollection of my school taking an interest in my language abilities. On that occasion, I was told to go to the special language unit at the top of the spiral staircase. Although there was great adventure in being released from ordinary class work, I remember entering that room with trepidation. The children already there were involved in what I would later come to recognize as basic phonics. Even as a child I remember feeling strongly that the test I was given was well beneath my capabilities. I came back down the spiral staircase, smugly satisfied with myself for having amazed the tester with my use of the word 'disguise'.

I tell this story to illustrate the feeling I have had ever since, that the abilities of bilingual children should never be underestimated. It seems to me that the qualities and insights of child interpreters are not celebrated to the same degree that their language deficiencies are highlighted.

Pursuing this issue, I undertook a project to investigate the perceptions of pupils, parents and teachers, of the roles taken by child interpreters at home and school. Some fifty-two people, in all, were interviewed in the West Midlands and the North East of England, and these included twenty-four school pupils from primary and secondary schools; seventeen parents; eleven teachers. The language of our conversations was that preferred by the interviewee, either English or Punjabi.

Page after page of transcription revealed that bilingual children acting as interpreters operate within a complex system of inter-personal relationships, attitudinal considerations and linguistic sleight of hand (or tongue). It is these which I want to consider now, within the categories of:

- Contexts and effects
- Family relationships
- Burdens
- Power
- Language insights
- Social skills.

CONTEXTS AND EFFECTS

Doorstep interpreting to parents for sales representatives was by far the most frequently reported. Among the house visitors were double-glazing people; evangelists (such as Mormons, Jehovah's Witnesses); gas and electricity officials.

As for public services, boys and girls translated and interpreted at hospitals, clinics, doctors' and dentists' surgeries, opticians, schools, solicitors' offices, advice bureaux, parental work-places, and even High Commissions. They also interpreted over the phone and were accustomed to dealing with explanations about various media (such as television and radio), and various kinds of literature (such as DIY home improvement manuals).

They interpreted on behalf of relatives, older people in the community, and even strangers in the street. Many were involved in buying items, and these could range from groceries to a car, or even a house. Obviously, such a list could be endless, but dealing with anything, ranging from a throw-away comment to social events, domestic arrangements, business matters, police crises, was within the experience of many children.

Having such a wide range of early experience inevitably had its effects upon the children. Having interpreted information, many child interpreters became accustomed then to being asked to make decisions. Hence, when they considered it appropriate, they bypassed interpretation for their parents and simply made independent decisions. So, when asked if they would refer to their parents over a doorstep domestic issue, no less than two-thirds of the children interviewed said that they made decisions independently. As one (Harminder) put it:

> I tell them straight. Sometimes the English person asks for your parents, but you know they're not going to be able to speak English, so you just pretend they're not in, and answer yourself.

Likewise in the family shop, Kushwinder took on a role more senior than that of her mother. After all, she was the one called on to deal with awkward customers. She spoke of:

> sorting out problems in our shop like when customers get narky, and argue over what they reckon is wrong change.

Such responsibility had its effects. As interpreters, children exercised discourse control; language censorship was at their personal discretion. They sometimes abused their privileged position for purposes of self-defence and manipulation. Thus Meena said:

> I would pretend my school report wasn't as bad as it was. I would pretend the teacher had told me to buy or do certain things, knowing my parents couldn't easily check up on me.

But, if the power could lead to misuse, it could also lead to reward. For some boys and girls their interpreting skills brought them parental praise, material reward, justification for absence from their normal classroom work, and access to new, and often adult, places, information and knowledge. It could even have the thrill of an adventure. It did so for Hardeep, when he was called on to translate for the police and to ask his grandfather for permission to search his house, in pursuit of a robber at large in the area.

FAMILY RELATIONSHIPS

Substantial parental language dependency and increased child responsibility appeared to alter the normal parent–child relationships in terms of power and control, leading to a degree of role-alteration. As one parent (Joginder) commented:

> In the Punjab, parents don't need to involve children in decisions until they are much older. In England it is necessary to involve the children even when they are young, because there are some things that the parents don't know about.

Such a change in relationship could be seen in a very positive light. Some parents saw dependence upon their children, together with their children's willingness to assist them, as a strong indication of the family's closeness. They welcomed the development. Thus, Kuldip's father:

> We feel proud that the children are happy to represent us.

This reciprocal dependency was recognized as mutually rewarding. One interviewee (Jas Kirat) put it like this:

> Parents do a lot for their children, so I think it's not bad if children do something back for them. It makes them confident that 'I know these things and I'm helping my parents.' It probably brings the family closer.

Parents were aware of their inadequacies and some felt anger, frustration and resentment at the imbalance in normal dependency patterns. Rej's mother said:

> If I wasn't reliant on the children for communication, I wouldn't have to send people away from the doorstep, telling them to come back when the children would be at home. I would be able to deal with it, there and then.

And Balbir:
> Sometimes I say, 'Not just that. Ask this as well.' But they won't ask

twice. That's when I feel if I could only speak myself, I wouldn't bother with them, and I get angry at them. They say, 'You ask, then!' knowing, full well, I can't.

Without language parents would be constantly disadvantaged and anxious, as they acknowledged. Gurbax said:

It would be extremely difficult for me to function without the children.

Balbir admitted:
I do worry that, when my daughters marry and leave home, we will be out on a limb as far as coping with both spoken and written English.

Sarabjit's mother asked:
What is life when you can't speak to anyone?

This language barrier could lead to discrimination within the family. For example, Reena's monolingual Punjabi-speaking grandmother was patronized and ridiculed in English, in my presence, by both Reena's 7-year-old brother and her mother. As Reena's mother said about granny's rights:

It's not needed for her to know. You don't have to tell her. She never enters conversations anyway.

It could also lead to inter-personal sparring and manipulation, where participants, like dogged poker players, concealed their strengths and weaknesses. Witness this comment from Baljit's mother:

Every night when I was ten, with the Nine O'Clock News, my dad would say, 'Tell me what's going on in the news'. My dad is not a very calm person and he'll think he knows more, but he doesn't really. He'd keep saying, 'No. I don't think you're explaining that right. Tell me again.' He thinks he's clever. He'd say, 'I knew, really. I was only trying to help you out.' I would sit and listen to it all and then, afterwards, he would say, 'Just summarize it'. I'd tell him what he wanted or needed to know.

In some instances, relationships had deteriorated to a level involving differential treatment. As Charmaine observed:

Some of my friends swear at their mum real bad but, as soon as their dad comes home, they're quiet and real good.

How different it was in those homes where communication was well established. As one mother said:

I feel I get on better with my kids because we can all talk English. We don't have to wonder what they're talking about. You can't get close to your parents when they can't talk English. I have a better relationship with my children than my parents had with me.

On occasions, parents viewed child interpreters as self-surrogates and projected something of their own expectations on to their children. This was reflected through the content which some interpreters were expected to handle, as well as the emotional sensibilities and knowledge they were required to demonstrate. These expectations put pressure on parent–child relationships. Meena's sister-in-law said:

If I can't interpret, mum gets frustrated and says I should know because I was brought up here.

And Kuldip's father told us:

If they hesitate and stumble when interpreting, we say, 'What are we sending you to school for?'

Culturally, parents felt it was their children's duty to assist them. They regarded their own migration as the means of providing their children with an English education and, by way of return, expected help when it was required. In this respect, a kind of emotional and cultural manipulation was at work, which usually defeated children's initial resistance to interpreting. Joginder explained:

Sometimes children say, 'I'm tired. I'm fed up.' Then I feel a little bit angry that they won't do even a little job for me. I feel angry but then, afterwards, after they've cooled down, they come round again, perhaps because they think they didn't respond fairly.

Some children actually took on the role of acting as instructors in Punjabi to their teachers, and instructors in English to their parents. Jaswinder, for instance, recounted:

Mother said, 'When you come home from school, you'll have to learn me.' I tell her little words first. I tell her, this means this; this means that. Next morning I ask her about it. Next I'll teach her how to read books, then harder books.

Sometimes the tables could be turned, as Gurmit reported:

My gran was a pukka Punjabi speaker and my mum had to help me out. It was funny. I felt inferior to them. Normally, it would be me who would be saying, 'No, this is wrong', and so on and so on. Then, they were telling me.

In the manner of many teachers, too, some bilingual children, defying cultural norms, assumed the superior and knowledgeable position of acting as appraisers of their elders' English, as reported by Rupinder:

> Sometimes when she's writing a letter for school, she makes silly mistakes like 'can't', when it should be 'could', and so I tell her. Sometimes she does it again. Other times she won't change it when I tell her how to do it.

And Gorma recounted:

> When we had a sales representative come, my mum was being taken in by them, when she should have been saying, 'We've had one before and we don't really like this magazine'. She wasn't making a very good job of it.

Another way of expressing one's superiority during interpretation is to adapt the message and style to what one considers more appropriate. I do this myself. When interpreting on behalf of my own mother, I sometimes make judgements about the way she is presenting herself and if I feel, for example, that she is being too humble, I will not present this in my choice of words. I make judgements about the way she organizes her language and what she wishes to convey to another person and I become frustrated by any perceived inadequacies. I often make judgements about her message clarity, about the appropriateness of what she is saying, about the manner in which she expresses it. When I interpret for her, it is in my power to modify both the medium and the message, and I do.

BURDENS OF INTERPRETING

However, alongside the pleasures of feeling superior, there were also, for some, the pressures of being exposed, of having to take the initiative and of being regarded as an expert. Thus, Pindy recorded:

> I felt as though I was under the spotlight.

Kushwinder complained:

> Sometimes I feel a bit shy and feel stupid, that I don't want to go up to people and talk.

Harminder explained:

> Teachers think that, because you can speak Punjabi, you will be able to explain it quite nicely, but sometimes it is difficult to find the right

words in Punjabi, and it is hard to explain things to your parents and that puts a lot of pressure on you.

This pressure was experienced not only in the problem of finding appropriate language alternatives, but also in the roles which the interpreters were called on to play prematurely. As mediators of adult interactions, they often found themselves bearing the emotional and psychological brunt of the interaction, too. Nerinder, for instance, spoke of having to deal with the frustrations and anxieties caused by misunderstandings on either side. Hardeep resented having to make relationships among his grandfather's peer group. Kushwinder was concerned that the English speaker might attach less weight to what was said by the monolingual Punjabi speaker because it was said via a child.

In addition, there were some issues of adult concern which were too difficult for children to understand, such as picking a way through the social security benefit laws or the legal niceties of buying and selling a property. Other issues were inappropriate for children on account of the delicacy of content. Into this category might come matters of parental personal health. There was a fear that children might get things out of all proportion and suffer unnecessary emotional stress. Nerinda was disturbed, for instance, when, on behalf of her mother, she had to discuss matters about:

> the vagina and stuff, when I was about ten. She (mother) had to say these things and I don't think she wanted me to know really. I felt embarrassed in front of my mum. It was on my mind for a few weeks. I felt I was a bit too young to know about those things.

Occasionally, the whole thing could get out of hand with potentially disastrous results, when the burden would become absolutely intolerable. Such instances, while rare perhaps, would be long-lasting in their effects. Such was the case with Balbir's son, as she explained:

> Sometimes, when interpreting, the children do make their own decisions about things and pressurize us into agreeing with them. This was the case when my son invited a video-hire representative over the phone to the shop, and was taken in by the persuasive talk and then urged us to hurriedly sign a contract to say we would stock their videos.
>
> It later turned out that they kept leaving us with old videos that we couldn't get rid of. This led to legal action and a lot of arguments with the video company. When we explained that we couldn't understand English very well, our solicitor asked us how it was that we could run a shop and yet not be able to check the details of a contract before signing.

My husband then made our son make threatening phone calls and write rude letters to the firm. My son was in a great deal of trouble over the whole matter.

POWER

It will have been evident throughout this chapter, and not merely from Balbir's story, that being an interpreter carries with it a great deal of power. Whoever commands the language commands the power. In such a situation, children and parents reverse roles; the former are in control and the latter dependent. Harminder expressed this with great clarity:

It does make you powerful, because you always know something before them and you have to pass it down to them, whereas, usually, it's them passing information down to you. It makes you feel good, knowing, 'I know now but I have the choice of whether I want to tell them or not'.

One teacher reflected Harminder's views precisely:

There is a definite increase in power, and the position of the child in the family, because they are given responsibility and access, and access is power. They can communicate directly and the parent can't ... You can see the parents are hanging on what the child is saying. That is their life line to what is happening.

Naturally, the extent of child power is in proportion to the level of language knowledge possessed by parents or others. Parvinder explained it thus:

My mum knows a little English and if I didn't tell her the right thing, she would know if I was lying, so I'd have to tell her.

Correspondingly, in school, pupil power to exclude the English-speaking teacher decreased in relation to the limitations of the child's Punjabi, or was dependent on maintaining deceptive body language. Kulwant had some difficulties in this respect, and reported:

Sometimes from the giggles going on, monolingual English teachers can tell that the girls are not on task, but discussing something else.

Parents, as teachers, pick up such signals. Some, like Gurbax, have implicit faith in their children:

I always trust that they do interpret faithfully ... They interpret whatever I say and anything additional that is necessary for them to add.

Others are less trusting. Witness Sarabjit's mother:

> Afterwards I have to ask them, 'Did you say more or less than I asked you to?' There's nothing to compare with being able to speak the language yourself. There's always an element of doubt as to what's understood. Sometimes I have to prepare the children beforehand, telling them to interpret only what I say, and to say nothing of their own accord.

In fact, it was clear from the pupils' comments that they did alter messages during the process of translation, as has already been indicated. Sometimes it was because it was felt improper to ask what parents were requesting ('Ask him if those tomatoes are ripe'); sometimes it was through lack of interpreter knowledge; sometimes there was deliberate distortion, if accurate translation was not in the interpreter's best interests.

LANGUAGE INSIGHTS

Interviewee responses revealed a whole wealth of language experiences and awareness on the part of child interpreters. At a basic level, for instance, bilingual boys and girls were aware, very early on, of the existence of various languages: Urdu, Gujarati, Hindi, English, Punjabi.

Building on such awareness, interpreters were able to bypass lexical limitations and use a variety of strategies to effect communication, including lexical parallelism; mime and gesture; straight definitions. Nerinda explained:

> If I don't know what a Punjabi word means, I have to ask my mum. Then she explains it in different words.

Gorma went one stage further:

> If I was writing something in Punjabi and didn't know what it meant, I could ask someone for the English word.

Such code-switching or language supplementation gave boys and girls direct experience of the fact that no one language can ever fully parallel another. For example, at the age of just 11, Meena realized that sometimes puns do not translate effectively. Simita commented:

> There are certain phrases that you can only use in English, and certain things you can only understand better in Punjabi.

Pindy asked herself the key question which interpreters must constantly put to themselves:

> I ask, 'Would that word really mean that?'

Some parents pointed out that children's exposure to adult use of language enabled them to discover new syntactical and lexical structures. Moreover, where children did not know the strict translation of a word, the need to interpret led them to discover the word required, thereby increasing their vocabulary. This particular point was made by Baljinder, Joginder Surinder, among others.

Simita was aware of the difference between the ability to produce or receive a language, and of what her own abilities were in two languages.

Ten-year-old Reena was aware of the notion of accents, and the need to alter grammatical structures when translating information into a different language. She was also sensitive to her mother's shortcomings in importing Punjabi linguistic rules into her production of English:

> It feels funny because they have a different accent in speaking, and a different ending. Then everybody laughs if she says something wrong.

Harminder was aware of different modes and varying levels of language difficulty. She explained:

> They don't use basic language on the News, but adult language like 'international'.

Manjit appreciated something of the aesthetic appeal of a language:

> Poetry writing would be easier in Hindi. I think it's a really sweet language, sweeter than Punjabi. You can express yourself better than in Punjabi.

Kuldip commented on how language switching occurred:

> I sometimes speak Punjabi in the playground, because sometimes out of my mouth comes a Punjabi word, and then we all carry on speaking Punjabi.

In the course of handling adult interaction, child interpreters experienced various discourse types and became familiar with the kind of information that needed to be exchanged in certain contexts. Thus, Gorma seemed to have become quite skilled in the art of interpreting, and aware, from experience of customary questions, of the kind of information needed by both sides in certain situations:

> I would propose that we ask certain relevant questions to find out main points like the guarantee, the quality, the price.

Likewise, Harminder was aware of the unspoken rules that govern particular discourse types. She realized, for instance, that, during an interview with a solicitor, it is the solicitor who assumes the prerogative of deciding discourse direction, in order to obtain relevant information in a structured way, and also to maintain control of the exchange.

Interpretation, then, is a two-way process and the interpreter acts as intermediary, sometimes responding to questions, sometimes acting on instructions, sometimes taking a more independent line. It is not surprising, in all of this, that the very act of being an interpreter involves a degree of empathy. Nerinder captured this quality in her comment:

> Some English people don't like it if you speak Punjabi. On a bus there were two English people sitting behind two Indian women who were speaking Punjabi. The English man was saying to his neighbour, 'How dare they speak this? They could be speaking about me. It's rude. I wouldn't speak another language.'
>
> I felt like telling him, 'You are speaking another language. They can't understand.'

She is clearly accustomed to the idea that, if people are not members of a particular speech community, then the use of that language in their presence could present an alien threat.

Likewise, ten-year-old Hardeep displayed empathy with the needs of other language users through his deliberate decision to speak the language understood by all present. One could see in his choice valiant endeavours to assess and match the most appropriate language in the circumstances, depending on speakers' needs and preferences.

Similarly, Manjeet, who revealed an impressive appreciation of the speech process of the emergent second-language-speaker, and how to aid memory, fluency and expression through the use of cues and key words, said:

> They know what they want to say. They say a few words, forget what they want to say, so I give them the start of it and they finish it.

In such ways, not only are interpreters developing the quality of empathy, they are also, it appears, developing their own conceptual grasp of events and issues. After all, command of two languages must equip an individual with some access to a minimum of two ways of thinking. If one believes that one language can never be absolutely paralleled by another, it must follow that the bilingual person has access not only to two perspectives of a concept, but also to the interaction of those two concepts. They rehearse notions in two languages but the very fact of such rehearsal may represent, in itself, aspects of a third way of looking at the world. Manjit hinted at this:

> When you're doing something in Punjabi and a word comes across

which is similar in Hindi, it makes you think in Hindi and the two languages combine together to make you learn better.

SOCIAL SKILLS

As a result of acting on behalf of adults in adult situations, young interpreters experience knowledge and places prematurely. Kuldip's father spoke of 'going into offices as a new experience for them'. Meena pointed out how she realized it was necessary to sign for registered letters. Nerinda felt that, through accompanying her mother to the doctor's surgery, she learned the purpose of certain medicines.

Many of the situations which young interpreters handled led to increased maturity, astuteness, assertiveness and self-reliance, born of early adult experience. Provided that children were able to cope with it, exposure to adult responsibilities appeared to be a morale-boosting experience. In their capacity as interpreters, most children felt a sense of privilege, value and satisfaction which enhanced their self-image. As one parent put it:

> It could help them become confident through helping other people, increase their self-esteem and learn to stand up for themselves more.

The children, themselves, gave similar testimonies. Nerinda declared:

> I feel as though I'm the one with all these responsibilities. I'm the one who has to do things and tell people things. I feel good, then. I feel powerful.

And Gorma:

> I feel good and proud of myself. A little bit clever.

It seems that Gorma has also experienced that little thrill of pride which I felt on the spiral staircase years ago.

Appendix 8

Bilingual policy guidelines

These notes are offered as a prompt to any group of staff charged with the responsibility of developing and implementing a bilingual policy for their school. Such a group might wish to consider this series of questions, assertions and practical ideas, under the headings of:

Who? (Who is involved?)
Why? (Why have a bilingual policy?)
What? (What practical activities might take place?)

WHO IS INVOLVED?

Clearly, any bilingual policy will have some effect on all children, parents and professionals in the school. However, the children most directly concerned will be those whose mother tongue is not English. (The term is used here synonymously with 'home'/'community'/'heritage' language.) They are referred to as 'bilingual' or 'developing bilingual'.

In fact, the term 'bilingual' is often used loosely and inaccurately of a group of people with a variety of abilities. It has come to refer to dual-language users in inner-city schools. Such application disguises a complex range:

- Some bilingual children may have high-level oracy and literacy skills in two or more languages;
- Some may have a basic oral command in one language, with more developed skills in another;
- Some may have fluency in two or more languages, but selective use according to setting (e.g. playground/classroom) or function (e.g. personal/academic).

We can easily make the mistake of assuming fluency, when we do not understand what is being said. It is crucial, then, to do as detailed a survey as possible of individual and group needs. Appropriate planning, grouping, teaching and assessment depend on accurate information.

WHY HAVE A BILINGUAL POLICY?

There are four main reasons.

(a) It acknowledges the presence in school of certain children with abilities which should be recognized, as a means of supporting the self-esteem of those children; of aiding their intellectual and academic development; of giving them recognition within their community and perhaps enhancing their life chances.

(b) It should lead in school to an increase in awareness of language and languages; to an acknowledgement and acceptance of cultural diversity; to greater communication between members of various cultural groups.

(c) It promotes notions of the integrity and value of all languages and dialects, stressing the active involvement of children in genuinely communicative situations, and the inter-dependence of any two or more languages possessed by individual people.

(d) It will assure parents that mother tongue is not being developed at the expense of English, but that each is complementing the other, to the benefit of the child.

WHAT PRACTICAL ACTIVITIES MIGHT TAKE PLACE?

Suggested activities fall into three groups.

(a) Cross-curricular activities, using mother tongue to develop concepts and enhance its status/value in the children's eyes, may include:

- re-telling of stories by children;
- role play (perhaps with puppets);
- sequencing/cloze/caption-writing/matching;
- discussion preceding curriculum activities;
- book-making (perhaps of an ancestral homeland visit);
- audio tape-recording (perhaps in the playground);
- singing songs and rhymes;
- using mother tongue in assembly;
- making multilingual school notices;

(b) Learning English through the medium of mother tongue, with bilingual colleagues, can proceed by means of:

- acting as communicators to translate lesson content/practise language patterns/develop vocabulary;

- producing/translating books in English and mother tongue, written and illustrated by the children;
- discussing items from ethnic minority newspapers;
- compiling a multilingual anthology or magazine, to include stories/jokes/reports/interviews/advertisements.

(c) Language awareness topics may involve, for example:

- language questionnaire (to children and staff);
- graph construction (showing language distribution);
- autobiographical writing about oneself and family;
- vocabulary of family relationships;
- collection of language scripts;
- survey of languages in the immediate environment;
- mapping of languages represented in the class;
- invitations into school of local bilingual speakers.

Chapter 7

Teachers speak out
Bimla Sidhu and Richard Mills

EDITORS' INTRODUCTION

In many parts of this book, the voice of individual developing bilingual children is heard (as it is in Grugeon and Woods, 1990), whether in class, playground, home, or elsewhere. The premise behind this approach is that we can learn as much, if not more, from the words of real (if disguised) boys and girls, as we can from a combination of graphs, charts and statistics. Or perhaps we learn in a more direct, vivid, engaging, personal, affecting manner.

This time it is the turn of bilingual teachers to say what they feel about bilingual education for children; about their own bilingualism; about their perceived status within the school and community; about their professional training and promotion prospects.

Initially, the picture presented is optimistic, with valuable individual testimony as to the positive benefits of bilingual education for particular children, and to the value for those children of identifiable role models. However, there are indications of much tension just below the surface and this is seen most strongly in comments made about professional development and promotion. Those interviewed wished to be regarded, above all, as competent teachers who happened to have an additional skill, i.e. bilingualism, just as it might have been music, or drama, or games. They wished to be able to gain promotion in the same manner as any other colleague, and not to be diverted away from mainstream, not to be, as they saw it, marginalized into a supporting role.

With this in mind, they felt that their bilingualism, while undoubtedly a prized asset, was not be regarded as an exotic aberration. As one says, displaying a modest confidence shared by few monolingual people, 'Anyone can learn another language. I don't feel extra special because I know Punjabi.'

The general approach of this chapter recalls that of Amrit Wilson in her impressive book *Finding a Voice* (Virago, 1978). Both that book and this chapter give us the opportunity to listen to voices rarely heard.

I think there is a tendency to pigeon-hole Asian teachers into doing or knowing all about languages faiths and cultures of children in their schools. How many monolingual teachers know about Burns Night or other festivals?

(bilingual infant teacher)

This chapter is based on the views of ten bilingual teachers (see Appendix 9). It is, thus, no large-scale, comprehensive and definitive piece of research. Rather, it presents an opportunity to hear the views of individual members of the teaching profession talking about:

- Multilingual approaches in the classroom
- Children's attitudes to mother tongue
- The roles of ethnic minority teachers
- Professional development.

The views expressed are not necessarily representative, but neither are they insignificant or irrelevant. What they offer is a window through which monolingual teachers may glimpse something of the professional world of bilingual colleagues.

This professional world includes bilingual children who may not, themselves, belong to a homogeneous group. These children may be orate and literate in one or more languages, or in the very early stages of learning. They may be members of long-established communities, or semi-detached from a shifting, unsettled population. They, and their families, may be strict adherents to a great religion, or ignorant of such matters. They may be found in multilingual, multicultural classrooms, or attend predominantly monocultural schools.

In these, and other, respects such bilingual children are like their monolingual peers and, ideally, need to be regarded as individual people, not as fodder for stereotyping. It is the same with teachers. We have much in common, but our experience is unique.

MULTILINGUAL APPROACHES IN THE CLASSROOM

All ten interviewees said that, wherever possible and appropriate, they used the children's mother tongue, as well as English. They had made a conscious, professional judgement to do this, as a means of building on home experience and developing both languages simultaneously.

Teacher 4, for instance, uses Urdu, Punjabi and English, and finds a ready response with very young children. She reports:

> I found Nursery and Reception class children who only had mother tongue and not much English. In that situation you're a real asset to the children. They feel more secure and at home when they see someone they can identify with. They more or less cling to you; you are the only familiar thing there. They can open up to you, whereas before they may be more quiet ... It's useful to have even a monolingual teacher who can speak a few words or sentences at the early stage, in a language familiar to the children. For example, simple commands, numbers, or colours. That goes a long way to helping children to open up to you. It makes the transition easier from home to school, don't you think?

Teacher 2 endorses this view and develops it by stressing the balance that can be achieved between mother tongue and English. She says:

> I like to use the languages positively in the classroom. The reception class is an extension of the home, so it's natural for me to use both languages ... When the children come into the reception class they usually know some English, often just words. Their Punjabi is usually more developed; they can often speak more fluent sentences. Therefore, at this early stage, I am translating Punjabi words into English so that the children are familiar with the English equivalent. As they develop, their English vocabulary will do so, so that, by the time they are tops, they can often switch languages quite fluently.

This teacher, for obvious reasons, experiences nothing of the anxiety expressed by some monolingual teachers that they do not know what their children are saying. She regards the dual-language context as normal and to be expected. She is aware of differential development in her children but is confident that, given time, their ability in both languages will be satisfactory.

Progress in English can sometimes appear disconcertingly slow but, when teachers look back over several months of a child's being in school, they realize how much has been accomplished. (For instance, within nine months of starting school in England from Bombay, 10-year-old Vivek, from another class, habitually joined in class discussions; produced his own topic booklets; asked for extra work; talked with friends in the playground – all in English.)

For Teacher 2, language acquisition and development is a two-way process, with each language benefiting from the other. As she says:

> I switch words that they do not know for the other word. I try to ensure

that I'm using the equivalent, so that I'm not just concentrating on Punjabi but English too. I want the children to use both languages easily. The only way they can do so, is if *you* can use both languages easily.

Teacher 5 is able to call upon five languages from her own repertoire: Punjabi, Urdu, Pushtu, Bengali and English. She uses all with her children, not only for reinforcement, but also as a means of helping them to learn small pieces of another language, thereby developing their concept of language variety among their peers within the class. It is as natural a form of multicultural education as one could devise. She says:

Often we sing songs in the different languages. All the children have learnt to sing the song 'Peter and Paul' in Punjabi, Pushtu and Bengali, as well as English. Sometimes I am reinforcing the English language through Punjabi or Urdu. Sometimes I will issue instructions or commands in their mother tongue, that is, usually whole sentence structures. But I won't only say it to the bilingual children. Often I say to Gary, 'chup!' ('quiet') and he knows the meaning of the Punjabi. So, for me, using another language is not only with bilingual children but with all children.

Teacher 9 was aware of the temptations to the children of selective listening and realized the danger that they might only respond when their preferred language was being used. As she observes:

I didn't want them falling into the trap. If they know you can speak Punjabi, they think there's no point in speaking English. But that's not how bilingual education functions. It's a matter of one language reinforcing the other. So whatever I said, I would try and reinforce it. I didn't allow one language to dominate. I made sure the children were listening equally so they didn't switch off when it came to the English. When the children spoke, they would offer me some Punjabi and I would coax out the English.

The word 'coax' indicates something of the sensitivity involved in such teaching, where a careful balance needs to be maintained between the two languages and where encouragement is crucial. As she goes on to say:

I never forced it out of them. As long as they felt comfortable, it didn't matter if they said it wrong or just said a word. As long as they had a go and tried.

This conscious and positive use of multilingual skills reflects the most up-to-date thinking in this area, where a partnership of languages is promoted and each is used for the genuine development of the other. It is light years away from earlier thinking, touched on in the Introduction to this book, when the classroom was regarded as precious English-speaking territory and other language intrusions were summarily dismissed. Teacher 1 remembers that time:

> In the beginning, it was presumed that 'immigrant children', as they were called then, would pick up English if they spoke or heard English. Allowing them to speak their own language in school would be detrimental educationally. Of course, they had to know English if they were going to live or stay in England. So the policy in some of my earlier schools was 'no Indian or Pakistani in the classroom'.

The same policy at that time would have been reflected in the provision of books, with only English texts being available. However, the present approach is one of respect for a variety of scripts alongside, or in addition to, English.

Teacher 4 reflects this common experience:

> Where possible, we translate notices for our parents' board. The Welcome poster is in various languages. We include library books in mother tongue and English; books solely in mother tongue, versions of well known stories; also books written in English, produced by ethnic minority publishing firms.

The issue of dual-text books mentioned here is worth a little more investigation.

Apart from the fact that those available are mainly fiction, and often for young children, there is little doubt that they provide very helpful material for language awareness work in giving a context through which all learners, monolingual and bilingual, can discuss aspects of unknown languages. Teacher 10 recognizes this feature when she says:

> I did some songs in Punjabi and I took in some dual-text books, but the texts weren't English and Punjabi. They were Chinese. I used them for exposure, just to make the children aware of other writings and languages.

However, the use of dual texts as offering complementary versions of the same story is not so straightforward as might be thought. Teacher 7 highlights the translation problem. He says:

> Most of the texts are translations of popular English books. If the translation is wrong, you get no message across, and the language is disjointed ... There's often a problem in terms of culture. Where is the

culture? For many people, language and culture are inevitably tied together.

Moreover, it is difficult, if not impossible, to accord each language equal status in a dual-text book. As Teacher 7 makes clear:

It's like the English text is important and the other one just added to it.

With home and school-produced dual texts:

Often the English is typed and the community language handwritten, so the status of the two languages in one book can be a problem.

In any event, why should a pupil, faced with such a book, read both texts? Perhaps at home a child would read one text and parents the other? Or perhaps the real advantage is not for the child at all, but rather for the monolingual teacher who will be able to follow a comprehensible version and thereby understand what bilingual children, or their parents, are reading.

Teacher 7's solution is quite simple:

With older children, perhaps it's better if you send two separate books home, one in English and one in the mother tongue. Then the parents think that's good, that the children are learning both languages.

CHILDREN'S ATTITUDES TO MOTHER TONGUE

Several teachers commented on the embarrassment of bilingual children in hearing or using their mother tongue in the classroom. Thus Teacher 2:

When I first started and spoke to the bilingual children in Punjabi, they just laughed at me. I think they were initially embarrassed at speaking in their mother tongue in front of their monolingual friends. So I explained that they spoke to their parents and grandparents in Punjabi, so why not with me? Afterwards they responded in whatever language they were spoken to in. Now they are fine. They speak to each other in Punjabi. I think before, because their teacher only spoke in English to them, they thought that was the only language they were allowed to speak in.

The moral from this is that children need to be reassured that the language of home has a valid place in school, and that the classroom can accommodate other languages than English, although such reassurance may take time, as Chapter 1 indicated.

Perhaps children's age and, more certainly, their previous experience, are important factors in determining attitude. Teacher 4, for instance, found that infants were far less inhibited than juniors. She recounts:

> Many infant children would, quite willingly, tell stories in their mother tongue, yet the juniors were reluctant, perhaps because they had not been encouraged to use their mother tongue in the early years.

It took time for the bilingual children in this class to come to regard their bilingualism as an asset in their story-telling and story-writing projects. The breakthrough, then, was all the more rewarding when it did occur. Teacher 4 again:

> I remember one child, in particular, who moved from a previous denial of his bilingual skills to a willingness to use those skills for story telling and for general communication purposes. He often went down to the Infants Department to read stories to the children.

The initial reluctance, which took time to overcome, was not surprising to this teacher. In fact, she expected it, especially as:

> I've even come across bilingual teachers who have been reluctant to use their mother tongue in the classroom. They loathed to volunteer their asset, or they pleaded ignorance of any language other than English. So, for me, finding out some children rejected their own language was not new. It was seen as a challenge for them to come to a sort of acceptance.

It is almost as though children and teachers need to accept the condition of being bilingual and regard it, not as a stigma, but a strength. Presumably, in each case there is the unwillingness to appear different and this is why a child will answer in English a question asked in Punjabi.

However, there may be other, more specific reasons and Teacher 9 feels she may have discovered one of these. She says:

> I noticed that the girls persistently spoke in mother tongue all the time, whether with themselves or an adult. Their language of preference was Punjabi, whereas the boys always spoke amongst themselves in English and when answering the teacher, regardless of whether the question was posed in English or Punjabi. I found out that these boys used Punjabi in their home, especially with their mum, but with their fathers they would fluctuate between either language, because the fathers were more confident in their use of English. It depends on parental attitudes and background, whether they value their mother tongue.

What of the reactions of monolingual children? Here teachers commented that while, at first, some mimicked and mocked their bilingual peers, this was merely an initial barrier which needed to be overcome. It could lead on to great benefits. Some children had their eyes and ears opened. For instance, in her story project, Teacher 4 found children who were unaware of their friends' bilingualism. She records:

> They began to become interested in the writings, pictures, texts of dual-language books. The most rewarding aspect of their story-writing project was when they went to the Infants Department and read their stories to younger children. They could see how their story in English was translated into another language by their friends.

Another teacher found similar interest in a monolingual infant school where she had decided to use Punjabi, even though no children could understand it. She began with bilingual stories, but soon found that the children wanted everything translated:

> They would say, 'Oh, Miss, will you say that in Punjabi? What does it sound like in Punjabi?'

On one occasion, after work on dual texts, one monolingual child wanted to write a bilingual story. Teacher and child worked on the book together, he writing in English, she in Urdu. Teacher 9 takes up the story:

> The next morning he seemed subdued. I questioned him and he said, 'My mum said I shouldn't be learning to write in Urdu. I should be learning to write and read in English.' I thought, 'Oh, no. What have I done here?' At the end of the activity he took his book home. The next morning he came back and said his mum and dad thought the book was really good. I knew his mum would be surprised that he had actually written a book, and it was a story the whole family had shared recently and she could relate to.

Clearly, in such risky endeavours, it is crucial to keep parents fully involved and informed, so that misconceptions are kept to the minimum.

THE ROLES OF ETHNIC MINORITY TEACHERS

Bilingual teachers from ethnic minority groups have more than their languages to offer to a school. Their cultural background and experiences often help other staff to focus on sensitive issues of race and ethnicity, and their very presence in the staffroom has an educative angle to it, for colleagues, parents and children.

They may often be required to act in an advisory capacity, but this role of 'expert' can be uncomfortable. As Teacher 1 points out:

We may know in depth about one faith and one language, but we do not necessarily know about all faiths and all languages. There are such vast differences between the north and south of India or Pakistan.

This wariness, and, perhaps, weariness, of responsibility is echoed by Teacher 10:

You feel that people are assuming more knowledge on your behalf, because you are Asian, than you actually possess. For example, I can speak and understand Punjabi, but I can't read and write it. People assume you can, and you almost feel an obligation that you should be able to.

Such responsibility sometimes involves mediation between school and parents of all backgrounds. On one occasion Teacher 8 was called on to talk with several white parents who had refused to allow their children to visit a Gurdwara. She recalls the details:

When I asked, 'Do you know about Sikhs?' a typical response was, 'Oh, yes. Are they the ones with turbans?' ... They weren't clear about temples or mosques. 'A temple, is that the dome-shaped one?' Or 'them white buildings.' Many parents said they thought their children were going to take part in a religious ceremony.

After explanation, the matter was resolved and the parents said, 'Oh, if we had known that, they would have gone. We thought it was indoctrination'. By which time, it was too late, at least for that excursion. However, it was not too late for the positive change in attitude which occurred when the parents had been fully informed, and when they had got to know this particular teacher individually, as a professional person concerned for their children's education.

Such contact reinforces the concept of ethnic minority teachers as role models, both for children and parents. Teacher 5 asserts:

I offer a breakdown of stereotypes. To many English children, Asian adults are only parents of their friends or the local shop keepers around here. So, hopefully, I am breaking down these images. To the Asian children I hope I am a stimulus or a role model, so that they are aware that Asian people can strive to certain positions of authority.

Where they are also female, so much the better, as Teacher 1 observes:

I think it is a good idea for the children and parents to see a head teacher and deputy head teacher, both females as well, from the ethnic minorities. We can serve as good role models and dispel preconceptions.

Such a positive role is as relevant in an all-white school as in one which is culturally diverse. Teacher 8 sees it as a means whereby racism may be combated. Teacher 9 regards it as a way of breaking down stereotypes. Her own experience confirms this view and she asserts:

> If you give a child a series of pictures of ethnic minority people, and you give them labels of professions, for example, teacher, doctor, dentist etc., I think you would rarely get a child who would label an ethnic minority person a teacher, unless they had had direct experience of that. Very few children have.

However, being a role model can bring its own pressures. Teacher 9, for instance, resents being regarded by colleagues merely as an interpreter. She looks for an equal and complementary role. Teacher 10 is uneasy that what she may say in Punjabi to parents may not be what her monolingual teacher colleague wishes her to say. Moreover, she feels a conflict in professional and personal roles brought on by uncertainty about how to use familiar and formal modes of address to parents. She analyses it thus:

> I introduce myself as 'Miss Sandhu' and keep the relationship on a title basis with parents. It is difficult when you are using Punjabi to them. For example, with a parent you feel obliged just to say 'tuhsi' ('you', respectfully) and just avoid using a name. You need to use the language positively but maintain a role also.

Teacher 5, on the other hand, values the close relationship brought about by a common language and culture. She says:

> Most of the Asian parents are fine. They can relate to me. They often call me 'Behnji' ('sister') and I often call them 'Behnji' or 'Bhaji' ('brother'). So there is a good rapport with parents.

She has not experienced the pressure exerted on Teacher 3 by parents with conflicting ideologies. Some parents wish her to be more English; some more Asian. She expresses it thus:

> There are parents, particularly the younger Asian mothers, who have perhaps been born and educated here, who stress the dominance of English, and have said to me that their children need English and the English way of life to survive in England. One mother went as far as to say that I should be more like the English teachers. I mean, I wear a saree, it's my dress. I shouldn't be told what to wear ... Older parents have shown me respect for wearing the traditional saree and have said that their children can relate to me.

Such were the expectations of some parents that this teacher had even been held responsible for Asian children she did not teach. She recalls a disciplinary incident involving a colleague.

> Sometimes, you may get the flak for no reason, apart from simply you are an Asian in authority. I distinctly remember an incident when an Asian mother came into school and started arguing with me over an earlier incident which had happened to her child. I didn't know anything about it, but this mum continued arguing that, as an Asian teacher, I was directly responsible for the welfare of Asian children ... Asian parents want you to fulfil a role of parent and more formal teacher; their expectations are going to be prominent.

Teacher 2 had experienced conflict in a different form, from parents who misunderstood aspects of English education:

> Some of the Asian parents have quite strict views about education. They've been educated in India, like me, where discipline is severe and the organization is different. There you read and write all day. There's no play. The parents don't see play or social activities as learning. They only see reading and writing as work.

This teacher had done her best to reassure parents but was doubtful about her success:

> I just explained, in Punjabi, some of the activities and play the children do and what sort of skills they are learning through jigsaws and games. I told them about some of the work the children would progress to in the year, but, to tell you the truth, I don't think they were convinced, although they were polite ... I think the parents are half afraid of airing their explicit views, because they think they will be rejected or regarded as criticizing the teacher.

In many ways, then, ethnic minority teachers are caught in between. They are, undoubtedly, role models, but what is the role? To judge from these comments, it is variously interpreted. To the parents, it seems to involve:

- exerting a strong parental responsibility, arising from cultural expectations;
- acting as a sounding-board and confidante, on the basis of shared pedagogic understanding;

To the teachers themselves, it seems to involve:

- exercising an appropriate professional responsibility towards all pupils, irrespective of their cultural background;
- mediating the English education system to sceptical parents and,

perhaps, acting as some kind of buffer between them and teacher colleagues.

Occasionally, surprises can occur which confound all stereotypes.

Teacher 1 regards herself as a minority teacher who does not look Asian. Parents often perceive her as a white teacher and, in consequence, will not speak to her themselves or do so, via their children, in English. She takes up the story:

> As soon as I said something in Urdu or Punjabi, parents would look at me in amazement and then, in English, say quite fluently, 'Can you speak Urdu, Mrs Hammond?' I would say 'Yes', and continue to speak in Urdu. From then on, parents would come in the classroom to talk about all sorts of things. Often enough I found that their English was quite good enough to get by with, but they were embarrassed and just used their children to translate.

An important point here is that this sense of embarrassment, and lack of confidence, goes a long way towards explaining why some parents appear unable and/or unwilling to visit school for parents' meetings. This is a source of frustration for many teachers (and, no doubt, parents also). The task of breaking down such barriers is a responsibility which all teachers, particularly those who act in a home–school liaison capacity, take very seriously.

PROFESSIONAL DEVELOPMENT

The majority of the teachers interviewed had done their teacher training abroad and there were clear differences between their experiences and those of the teachers trained in the United Kingdom. Such perceived differences would need to be validated by a much larger study, but certain points they made from their own personal experience are worth pondering.

Teachers from overseas, arriving in Britain, had been labelled as 'immigrant teachers' and it was assumed they would teach in 'immigrant schools'. Stereotyped judgements had been made about them, as Teacher 1 observes:

> In those early days, all teachers from abroad were all perceived to be the same. If one teacher had discipline problems, it was assumed that all teachers had these problems and therefore could not cope.

Each one trained in India and Pakistan had gone through formal retraining when they came to Britain and it was felt that the ability to maintain discipline had played a large part in their assessment.

Different methods, organization and resources had proved difficult for some, but the major problem had been employment, rather than training. Several felt that they had faced discrimination in their search for jobs. Teacher 4, for instance, had been advised to restrict her applications to inner-city schools and felt that, 'being Asian, you had to prove yourself more than normal'.

Teacher 6 had also felt ill at ease initially:

> I went to some interviews where I was rejected. They made me feel they were looking for a white person.

He had responded with resilience. He relates:

> I determined not to stagnate and not to be put upon. I am a highly motivated individual, one who likes to organize things, rather than have things done for him. You have to be confident of your own ability to do a job well.

He felt that, in terms of initial employment, the situation had improved a great deal since those early days. The problem he now identified was that of career development. 'There is a struggle to get promotion if you are black.'

Teacher 1 expressed this in a slightly different way. Speaking from her position as Deputy Head, she felt that ethnic minority staff were in danger of being marginalized, away from mainstream work. She claims:

> If an Asian teacher is seen to be popular with parents or developing community links, they are given the role of home–school liaison teacher. If good at multilingual issues they are pushed into being language support teachers. So, whichever, they are often moved from mainstream teaching into specific roles.

Other teachers recognized this situation and, while not at all devaluing specific support roles, felt that their work lay as class teachers with the stability of a physically permanent base and the responsibility for whole-class organization.

Those teachers trained in Britain had a very different perspective on employment opportunities. They had not experienced adverse discrimination in gaining teaching posts. Quite the contrary. Their additional strengths had been recognized. Their bilingualism, for instance, had been treated as a valuable asset in their initial training. As Teacher 9 puts it:

> College made a lot of difference. There was a lot of input into stressing

the child's mother tongue and developing it in differing ways. It has definitely raised my own awareness. I had never before valued my home language in the way we were encouraged to.

Likewise, Teacher 10 is quite clear about her position:

First and foremost, I am a general primary school teacher, who happens to be able to speak Punjabi. Just as someone else can play the piano.

This is echoed by Teacher 8:

I don't feel extra special because I know Punjabi. Anyone can learn another language. It's the attitude you take and how you employ it. How sensitive you are to it. We've got to develop our skills, whatever school and area we work in.

With regard to future recruitment of student teachers from ethnic minority backgrounds, those interviewed were of the same mind. They all felt that the status of teaching was not sufficiently high to encourage many entrants from Asian cultures. There was a time when teaching had been highly regarded, but not so now.

I think with a lot of Asian people, medicine, law etc. are of greater status than teaching. So if you've got academic potential, your parents mould you towards that more so.

Asian people don't see teaching as a profession. The family name is more established if you're a doctor, but teaching isn't seen in that light.

If my son said he wanted to be a teacher, I wouldn't object to it. But I'd rather he didn't.

There will, of course, be reasons other than low status which may act as a disincentive to entering the teaching profession. They include:

- low salary;
- stress;
- increased pressure from new legislation;
- adverse publicity.

To this must be added particular disincentives for members of ethnic minority groups, identified by Singh (1988), such as:

- absence of black teachers as role models;
- fear of racial discrimination and racial abuse;
- fear of being marginalized;
- lack of clear and consistent careers advice;
- lack of recognition of black teachers within the profession.

It all makes a pretty formidable list but, for those prepared to overcome these perceived obstacles, the rewards in terms of personal satisfaction are as great as they have always been in teaching. With many bilingual teachers of ethnic minority origin, there is an added ingredient, and Teacher 10 spells it out:

> I immediately felt, 'Yeah, I've got a skill for once which I can use and get credit for.'

In a similarly positive vein, Teacher 8 views language within the whole context of multicultural education which, in time, will simply be subsumed with the concept of 'good education'. She defines it as:

> Valuing the needs of all children, regardless of race, gender and social class, and catering for these needs sensitively. It's about sharing knowledge and experience with children. So teachers and children can learn from one another. It's about teachers finding out about children's faiths, languages etc. and equipping themselves with sufficient knowledge to be able to share in these children's experiences and relate to them. It's a celebration of everything a child brings with himself or herself to the class. Multicultural teaching is making use of that knowledge and applying it in the curriculum as a whole, to make learning meaningful to the children and to meet their needs.

Appendix 9

Details of interviewees

Teacher 1 Female Deputy Head of Infant School. Speaks Urdu, English, Punjabi.

Teacher 2 Female bilingual support teacher. Speaks Punjabi, English.

Teacher 3 Female bilingual support teacher in Junior/Infant School. Speaks Hindi, Punjabi, English.

Teacher 4 Female Junior School teacher. Speaks Hindi, Urdu, Punjabi, English.

Teacher 5 Female Infant School teacher. Speaks Urdu, Punjabi, Bengali, Pushtu, English.

Teacher 6 Male Secondary School teacher. Speaks Hindi, Urdu, Punjabi, English.

Teacher 7 Male community languages tutor. Speaks Hindi, Urdu, Punjabi, English.

Teacher 8 Female Nursery/Infant School teacher. Speaks Punjabi, English.

Teacher 9 Female Infant School teacher. Speaks Punjabi, Urdu, English.

Teacher 10 Female Nursery/Infant School teacher. Speaks Punjabi, English.

Chapter 8

A community project

Sandra Hamilton

EDITORS' INTRODUCTION

The last chapter in the book points quite deliberately towards the wider community in which any school operates. It describes in some specific detail a particular project which was designed to draw on the bilingual strengths of a variety of adults within the community, for the benefit of some five hundred children in their local school.

One notable feature of the description, which should be of comfort to most readers, is the details of ways in which parts of the project originally failed. We can learn as much, if not more, from our failures as from our successes and, in this instance, the ultimate success of the project owed a good deal to earlier disappointments.

At a time when schools are gaining more autonomy, when the balance of power is shifting from LEA to Governing Body, this account will offer a useful perspective on both the strengths and weaknesses of the organization and, in particular, the resourcing, of an innovative and interventionist community project.

The chapter will also be of interest within the context of a debate on accountability. How should/does a school:

- seek to do its best for all its pupils?
- involve local non-professionals in its language work?
- ensure an appropriate level of commitment and involvement by the teaching staff?
- draw on the strengths of home–school liaison links?
- make provision for special initiatives within its language policy?
- communicate information to parents and other interested adults within the community?
- monitor and evaluate a substantial and far-reaching languages project?

Some answers to these questions will be found in the pages which follow.

A community is a particular group of people or part of society who are all alike in some way.

Community is friendship that is created and maintained between people or groups who are different in some way.

(Cobuild Dictionary, Collins, 1987)

Language education does not stop at the school gate. Most parents and teachers are aware of the value added to the school curriculum by the centrality of the school as a community focus, and by the constant and consistent transfer of knowledge and experience that can result from an effective partnership between home and school.

In the case of bilingual support, it has been my experience that as much information as possible should be gathered concerning the situation in which the teaching programme will be developed. Over a number of years, I have initiated bilingual support programmes in response to a perceived need. Only after failing in my earlier attempts did I realize that I was proceeding on the basis of assumption, rather than fact. It is only through examination of our failures that we can proceed on the basis of greater knowledge, and an historical perspective can inform future action.

As a class teacher, I always valued insights into the lives and thoughts of my young pupils, gleaned from comments made by parents during formal, or informal meetings, usually in school. But later, as a peripatetic teacher of English supporting children who spoke English as their second, or third, language, I became more aware of my own lack of knowledge regarding the language socialization of the children I was teaching.

The Linguistic Minorities Project (1985) attempted to answer questions concerning the languages spoken by bilingual children, in diverse locations and contexts. A research project such as this is useful in showing the way, but it cannot provide evidence for any situation other than the one it specifically seeks to examine. As teachers of developing bilinguals we have a responsibility to acknowledge and inform ourselves of the linguistic repertoire of our pupils, and to understand something of the pattern of their language usage.

For several years, in my capacity as English support teacher I operated a language class for parents (although only mothers attended) in the small room allocated to me, apart from the main school building. I soon realized that, whilst mothers never went into the school, they looked forward to their daily language class, and appreciated the opportunity to meet together and to talk to one another in their own languages, as well as forming a relationship with me – a member of a different language community.

Their needs appeared to be comparatively simple. They wanted to learn enough English to communicate with their children's teachers, and to be able to cope with travelling on buses and attending hospital clinics. Shopping and visits to the local doctor posed no linguistic problem. The area, by this time, had become the home of both professionals and trades-people with whom they could communicate either personally, or through the offices of a friend or neighbour acting as an interpreter. But I found that parents really needed to be able to understand what the school stood for. They had little or no knowledge of the English educational system and, as parents were reluctant to enter the school, it appeared to me that teachers rarely spoke to them in school and hardly ever visited the home of a pupil. As a consequence, there was no continuity between the child-ren's experience at home and at school, and little understanding on either side of the children's competence as developing bilinguals.

At this time, teachers working in all local schools of my inner-city area were operating under difficult circumstances. The pupil population of primary schools changed frequently. Sometimes children attended for days or weeks and then left the area. It was difficult to build up a relationship with children or their parents, and almost impossible to plan a teaching programme for more than a few weeks in advance. Through increased contact with parents, it became clear that more information about the community itself, and the function of languages used within the community was necessary if appropriate provision for the educational needs of the children was to be made. I realized that I needed to be able to work with, and for, the community as well as the school, and made the decision to move to a post as home–school liaison teacher in a large primary school in the same area.

The school had approximately five hundred children in the infant and junior departments, plus a sixty-place nursery unit. I arrived in January to find that a group of six 16-year-olds from a nearby comprehensive school had recently begun a series of regular, weekly visits to the school as part of their community-based project work organized by the outreach worker attached to their school. They worked in pairs, telling stories and talking to children from Years 5 and 6, through the medium of their first language. There were three groups: Punjabi, Urdu and Gujerati.

By the fourth week of my new appointment, it had become obvious that the older children were not enjoying their visits, and gaining little in terms of experience to add to their projects. Examination time was ap-proaching and, after discussion with the outreach worker, it was decided to discontinue the weekly sessions. Together, we attempted to evaluate the project, to articulate its aims in terms of both primary and secondary participants, and to try to identify factors that might have contributed to its apparent lack of success.

We realized that the school staff, and the class-teachers involved, had not been given an adequate opportunity to talk about the project, to express any anxieties, or to 'opt out', if they so wished. As a result, class-teachers had become irritated when a proportion of the class was extracted, and then returned, disrupting the work of the rest of the class. In addition, the groups had to gather in separate corners of the school hall, as no other accommodation was available. The hall was used as a passage by staff and children moving around the school, so that there were constant interruptions. The lack of a private base for the sessions diminished the whole programme in terms of its status as a feature of school life.

Furthermore, the 'story-tellers' found discipline impossible. The younger children were excited, and there was no member of staff permanently in the hall. In addition, lack of overt support from staff meant that the 16-year-olds felt diffident about their weekly visits, and started to find excuses to miss them. We also discovered that there was a mismatch between the language, or dialect, spoken by the older pupils, and the junior school children. School records listed the first language of each pupil, but often this was not the language that the child actually used, when not in school. We needed to have much more precise information about the children's actual language repertoire.

The project, clearly, had potential, and could have been a valuable experience for both junior and secondary school pupils, but we had no joint statement of aims, or objectives, which could be referred to for the purposes of evaluation. We were also aware that we had each considered the benefit to our own pupils as being of prime importance. With hindsight it became obvious that, in setting up any such programme, the linguistic abilities of all the participants, and the sociolinguistic context in which the programme is to take place, must be fully examined and taken into account.

We decided to discontinue the joint programme, in view of examination and timetabling constraints upon the older pupils and, for some time, the active promotion of the use of community languages in school diminished. It soon became obvious, however, that many parents would welcome its reintroduction. At this stage, staff were still not generally in favour of the idea, and it was clear that their support would have to be won before attempting to proceed any further. A number of meetings were held and after full discussion with the head teacher, staff, and a group of parents, in which anxieties and reservations could be voiced, staff approval was given and preparations were in hand to set up another project.

This time, I attempted to cater for as many languages represented in the school as possible. It was arranged that the parents'/community room would be used for lessons, and that three highly literate parents, plus one full-time member of the school staff, would teach Urdu, Gujerati, Pushtu and Bengali, the languages spoken by most of the school population. No-one could be found, at that stage, to teach Punjabi, Cantonese or Arabic, which were languages spoken by fewer children.

This second project was still centred very much around story and topic work, although the Urdu group also concentrated on literacy skills. School staff were asked whether they would be willing to participate, and if so, to suggest the most convenient time for the children to leave the class-room. Once again, Years 5 and 6 were the participants and the scheme, this time, was obviously popular with both parents and children. There were no complaints from staff, who had been involved in all stages of planning, and who were able to teach intensive, small-group activities with the remainder of their classes whilst the language sessions were held.

However, there were still several obstacles which prevented this pro-ject from achieving any real success. The initiative was difficult to maintain, as I had to co-ordinate and organize the movement of children, as well as carrying out other school and community commitments as home–school liaison teacher. Also, the project lacked status as a feature of school life, primarily because the bilingual teachers were volunteers, (other than the one member of staff), and they occasionally had other commitments. The sessions, of one hour per week for each group, could be, at times, either irregular or brief.

One of the aims of the project was to enable children to function through their first language within the school setting, but as they were being removed from their classroom, and their normal timetable, this was unrealistic. The use of story and themes for discussion meant that only a narrow range of linguistic experience was being used.

The volunteers were, in fact, being asked to carry out a task that was expected of no other member of staff. They each had a group of up to twenty children at one time, but the children were all at varying standards of linguistic proficiency in their home language. In addition, some parents had requested that the children joined the Urdu group, when in fact their first language was Punjabi, or Sylheti. Other children used a dialect at home, and whilst the volunteers all came from the appropriate speech community, they used the standard variety of the language in school. Thus, the volunteers were in the position of having to vary the content of the language session in such a way that every child could participate. In practice, this meant that they were actually using English as the teaching medium, and the child's home language to illustrate a teaching point.

Further modification and refinement of the programme was vital at this stage, and I produced a discussion document for the staff, concerning the implementation of community bilingual support which would utilize paid instructors from the local community, and which would run alongside the normal school curriculum in the classroom. As home–school liaison teacher, I proposed to combine my knowledge of the community with my interest in language, in order to co-ordinate the scheme. But first, it was necessary to gain the support of the staff, for this new project.

The following issues were put forward for discussion with the entire staff, including administrative and non-teaching support staff, as being of immediate concern:

(a) Why did parents express a wish for children's first languages to be used and promoted in school, as well as in the community outside school?

(b) Would any parents object to their children learning through the medium of a community language?

(c) How could we achieve the best possible deployment of school resources for the benefit of children from minority linguistic groups?

(d) Did we really understand the specific linguistic and conceptual needs of the children? For instance, where a child appeared to have little understanding of mathematical concepts, was help needed with maths or with the language of maths? How could we find out?

(e) Which languages/dialects could the children understand or speak, and which did they actually use?

(f) How could we decide which languages should/could be taught? Should we attempt to cater for all children, which might involve eight or more languages, or should we cater for the majority?

(g) What staff/resources/funding would be available? Was there a role for a bilingual classroom assistant?

(h) How could we determine the ability levels of the children, in terms of academic potential and linguistic competence?

(i) Where should any proposed programme start? Pre-school (playgroup / mother and toddlers' group), nursery, infant or junior level?

Staff were asked to comment upon the proposal that, if bilingual support were to become an integral part of the school curriculum, there must be constant liaison between representatives of the Local Education Authority and the school, in order to ensure adequate resourcing. More importantly, however, any future project focused upon the community needed the status of an educational initiative, if it was to be taken seriously. School and community were equally vital and it was now acknowledged and accepted that if bilingual support was to be effective, objectives must be clearly identified, and the programme must be implemented with the full co-operation of teachers, pupils and their families.

It was suggested that the school should take responsibility for disseminating any information gained from our experience, and for raising the awareness of other schools in the local community concerning the value of using community languages within the classroom, and thus, by implication, within the normal school curriculum.

Ideas contained in the discussion document were accepted by the staff, with the two important provisos that the instructors should come from our local community and, therefore, be familiar with the children and their particular use of language, as members of the same speech community. Also that, since the scheme would probably employ instructors who did not hold qualified teacher status, they should receive support and training from the school staff on a regular basis. This last point was accepted as being the crucial element in demonstrating our commitment to the success of the project.

It was recognized that all teachers would need help in adjusting to a different way of working, and thinking, in the classroom, and a further proposal was that priority must be given to the provision of some means of support for teachers who did not speak pupils' home languages, but wished to be involved in the bilingual development of their pupils. (In practice, the fear that had induced this last proposal disappeared once the project was under way. Teachers, children and bilingual support teachers interacted well, since they were all known to one another, sharing knowledge and 'exchanging' words and phrases in use in normal classroom activity.)

Objectives were proposed; the types of strategy that might be used in putting the proposals into effect were discussed; evaluation techniques were examined. Teachers had obviously become far more aware of the need to recognize and actively promote their pupils' knowledge and use of other languages.

At this time, the rationale behind the project stemmed very much from the opinions and desires of parents, and the local community. As home–school liaison teacher, I was in the privileged position of visiting homes every day as part of my normal school commitment. I had made both formal and informal links with members of the community not directly involved with the school, and had contacts with all the statutory and voluntary services operating in the area. Comments such as, 'Children need to learn their first language, because they are not quite competent to speak, and to comprehend', were regularly expressed. Other parents argued, 'Children want to know their own culture and religion. They want to be able to talk to parents and grandparents, to be able to write letters to relatives in India and to keep in touch with family in India, to have something to be proud of.'

I was also a member of a community group which met once each month to discuss local affairs. This group had been invited to assist local city planners in compiling an 'Area Study', which was soon to be produced for the first time. The Study represented a new approach to local planning, and was to be updated annually. Its purpose was to describe initiatives and projects currently planned within the area, and to consider local issues and concerns. It also sought to outline opportunities for change. This was an extremely useful facility, as it meant that my own impressions of community need could be validated by needs identified throughout the area by other individuals and groups.

As a result of several meetings with members of the Planning Department, I was aware that there was a demand for the use of premises in the locality for supplementary education classes, and for bilingual support after school hours. In addition, local residents were questioning whether community languages should be taught in schools as part of the curriculum. It was felt that these languages would be far more use to Asian children than French, German or Spanish. It appeared that there was a demand from the local community for the facility that we intended to provide.

Discussion with parents of children from all age-groups throughout the school, during routine visits to their homes, indicated a favourable attitude towards my proposals. I managed to speak individually to at least one parent of each child in the nursery and, by questioning a few of the parents of reception class children, who then acted on my behalf in speaking to other parents, I concluded that there were no dissenting voices. All parents approached were willing to allow their children to take part in the project.

However, it also became clear that, whilst parents certainly wished their children to maintain their first language, there was a general consensus that proficiency in English was far more important for their children's educational prospects. Parents insisted, 'Their future actually depends on this language.' English was vital, they said, so that 'they can get jobs and communicate in England'. A survey of parents found that, whilst oracy in the first language was required, it was generally agreed that literacy in English was far more important for their future educational and employment prospects. It became necessary to reassure parents of the benefits to their children from participation in a bilingual support programme. Research studies have pointed out the wisdom of encouraging children to use their first language, particularly during the early years of schooling, if the second language is to be effectively consolidated. Projects such as

'Mother tongue and English teaching for young Asian children in Brad-ford' (1978–81) and recommendations from the Swann Report (1985) were cited in particular.

The scheme was eventually planned to start in the nursery unit, and the reception classes, gradually moving up through the school. It would have been unrealistic to attempt to cater for the entire school in the first instance, and also it was felt that these classes would lend themselves to extra personnel working alongside the teachers, because of the flexibility of the timetable and daily routine. An additional factor influencing this decision was that the teachers of these younger children were the most enthusiastic and willing to work with bilingual instructors, and one of them was, herself, bilingual.

However, I had become increasingly aware that parents and other volunteers could not be expected to participate in what was, effectively, a professional undertaking, without remuneration. A survey of the languages spoken in the school provided information concerning the languages to be taught and, therefore, the number of instructors to be employed, and I was able to apply for financial support from community funds available at the time for local initiatives. The application included a statement of aims, which were:

To support bilingualism within the normal school setting and thus:

(a) generate confidence for learning through acknowledging and respecting the validity of all cultures and languages;
(b) enhance self-esteem and self-image of children;
(c) promote cognitive, social and emotional functions attributed to the maintenance of the first language.

A broader aim was to establish within the school a truly multicultural ethos, which exposed all pupils to the cultural and linguistic diversity of the community in which they were living.

The application also identified the participants. Where possible, all linguistic groups would be catered for eventually, throughout the age-range from 3 years to 11 years. However, constraints concerning the level of funding expected, and allocation of resources, would mean that the programme would be implemented gradually, starting with the younger age-groups and feeding upwards, and teaching those languages most widely spoken within the school community first.

It would have been impossible to cover every language represented in the school, as my research into the children's linguistic backgrounds revealed the following information.

Children in the school originated from: Bangladesh, the British Isles, Cyprus, Hong Kong, India, Kenya, Pakistan, Tanzania, Thailand, Uganda,

Vietnam, the West Indies, Yemen. Between them, they spoke thirteen languages in fifteen different combinations: Arabic, Bengali (Sylheti), Cantonese, English, Greek, Gujerati, Punjabi, Pushtu, Pushtu and Punjabi, Sindhi, Thai, Vietnamese/Chinese, Urdu, Urdu and Dutch, Urdu and Punjabi.

Children in the nursery originated from: Bangladesh, the British Isles, Burma, India, Kenya, Pakistan, Tanzania, Uganda, the West Indies, Yemen. Between them, they spoke nine languages in eleven different combinations: Arabic, Bengali (Sylheti), English, Gujerati, Punjabi, Pushtu, Urdu, Urdu and Burmese, Urdu and Punjabi, Urdu and Pushtu, Urdu and Thai.

Whilst we were awaiting the outcome of the application for funding, it was decided that the school language policy should be rewritten, in order to include the new proposals. This meant that several salient, but controversial, issues could be included, and staff were invited to discuss linguistic diversity; the use of non-standard language forms; teaching English to speakers of other languages; bilingual support; as well as the implications for bilingual/bi-dialectal children as they developed reading and writing skills. The policy already addressed the issue of differences between written and spoken language, and provided some guidelines for marking and assessing children's work. We also emphasized the need for consultation with parents, and the importance of in-service training and experience in language teaching.

As I continued to work in, and with, the community, as home–school liaison teacher, I became convinced that the project would now be welcomed by parents, and there was no apparent dissent from staff. Indeed, there was some enthusiasm. In anticipation of obtaining funding, several parents were approached as potential instructors. These included two who had been involved in previous bilingual support schemes, and who had continued to come into school to help with school activities and to assist teachers. As they had given their services willingly, and had demonstrated an obvious commitment to the school, it was felt that they should have the opportunity to take part in the project, if they so wished. Between them, these two could cover Gujerati, Hindi, Pushtu and Urdu, and they also had a good command of both written and spoken English.

Instructors were still needed for Arabic, Cantonese, Bengali/Sylheti and Punjabi. Although other languages and dialects were represented in the school, parents wanted their children to learn the standard form, or the language of literacy used within their community, insisting that, 'By learning the standard language, children will be able to understand the literature and written form in books and newspapers, where standard language is used. They will be able to understand all the different people speaking the same language from different dialects.'

Eventually, instructors were found for Bengali and (Sikh) Punjabi, but it proved impossible to find anyone sufficiently literate in both English and their first language to be able to teach the other languages required, within the normal curriculum.

The application for grant aid was eventually approved and, although the level of funding was disappointing, we were able to go ahead and appoint our first bilingual instructors from the local community.

The aims of the project remained as set out earlier. The objectives defined a situation that, it was hoped, would arise as a result of the project. They were intended to contribute to longer-term goals concerning equality of educational opportunity for all pupils (both majority and minority groups), through the creation of a specific ethos within the school, and through a change in attitude, towards the school, on the part of children and parents, and towards the languages spoken in school, on the part of the school staff.

The objectives were also to be used as a simple measure of output of the scheme, which could be compared with the aims and potential outcomes. They were listed as follows:

(a) the creation of an explicitly multilingual ethos within the school;
(b) the development of a multilingual resource bank;
(c) increased involvement of the family with community facilities (the parents'/community room, and individual projects set up by the home–school liaison teacher, e.g. establishment of literacy classes in minority languages for adults);
(d) liaison and co-operation with linguistic communities, through a programme of home visits and community involvement on the part of the home–school liaison teacher and other school staff.

During the first year of the project, the overriding consideration was finance. In theory, materials used for community projects should have been funded separately from those used in school. However, as the project was to take place within the school, it was agreed, after negotiation with the head teacher, that all expendable materials could be taken from school stock. Nevertheless, funds needed to be carefully managed. In other words, instructors could only be employed for the number of hours for which funds were available and, initially, we were only able to employ the three instructors for four hours per week. One hour was to be a training session, and it was this feature that proved to be most crucial to the project.

The instructors were based in the parents'/community room when not actually working with children, during which time they worked in the normal classroom environment, and they were free to use any facilities. Their training sessions were also to take place in the P/CR. Initially, I undertook these sessions myself, and I used the one hour per week available to familiarize the instructors with teaching techniques, such as the use of visual aids; different types of questioning; encouraging children to explain ideas to other children; how to promote an activity-based programme, focused upon the work already planned by the class teacher.

We discussed the importance of lesson planning and the necessity of being well prepared before each lesson began. Class and group management needed to be addressed, and we examined the results the instructors had found in handling the children in different ways. For instance, they had discovered very quickly that the children responded better orally when they were arranged in an informal grouping with the instructor seated at the same level as the children. Time was also spent discussing the opportunities and difficulties of collaborative teaching.

Materials were developed, both for the instructors' own use, and in response to requests from other members of staff. These included parallel scripts for displays and books; translations of safety instructions; exhibitions of food, together with the cooking implements (named) which were used to produce it; collections of authentic resources, such as items of clothing, musical instruments, books and newspapers and artefacts used during the major festivals of Eid and Divali, which the instructors brought from their own homes, or which they encouraged the children or their parents to bring in to school. Instructors needed time and advice in order to be able to produce the large, bold script necessary for display purposes.

Members of staff with responsibility for reading and maths organized some training sessions concerning the approaches and resources used in teaching literacy and numeracy throughout the school, and the instructors shared their experiences at staff meetings.

Nursery staff and reception class teachers were the first to receive assistance from the instructors. Each member of staff was given a record showing the languages spoken by children in their class, and asked to consider the areas of the curriculum where a specific instructor could be most useful to particular children. Instructors received lists of the children's names, and were advised that, although teachers would probably request help initially with children experiencing some linguistic or conceptual difficulty, they should work with any child in the class who approached them for help.

In this way, it was hoped that community languages would be accepted as a feature of normal classroom life, and would not be represented as appropriate only to a small and specific group of children.

Liaison with other members of staff proved to be one of the most significant constraints. As instructors were in school for such a short period each week, and because they could only be paid for the hours they actually worked, and not for 'talking time' with staff, I had to undertake to plan the weekly timetable for each instructor, in consultation with teachers, and make sure that each instructor was prepared for the lessons they were to teach. At times, this included gathering resources together and reorganizing timetables so that facilities were available for activities such as music, dancing or cooking.

Each member of the school staff, whether working with an instructor or not, and each instructor, received a copy of the 'Job description for instructors in community languages', reproduced below:

Instructors will draw upon a high personal standard of education and literacy in order to contribute to the linguistic and conceptual knowledge and literacy of children, through a particular community language.

1 Each instructor will contribute to the development of a resource bank directed towards bilingual support within the classroom. Resources may be used by the class teachers, or by the instructors with groups of children, and will include:
(a) stories on tape
(b) concept charts (numbers, colours, shapes etc.)
(c) collections of stories, rhymes, jingles, music, books, pictures and artefacts from various cultures.
2 Writing of parallel scripts for display boards, notices, information etc.
3 Liaison with both bilingual and monolingual staff members, in order to promote awareness of language differences, and similarities, and suggest methods and means of supporting bilingualism in the classroom.
4 Instructors will undertake a programme of group work with children in the classroom, either following a scheme devised by the class teacher, or following a complementary scheme devised by the instructor with the support of the teacher.
5 Development of schemes in drama, music and dance.
6 Weekly training sessions will be held for the purpose of pooling and expanding ideas, and developing practical instruction techniques.
7 Close liaison with the head teacher and with the home–school liaison teacher (co-ordinator), will be necessary at all times.

This not only set out the type of activity that the instructors would be involved with, but also indicated the professional status accorded to them, which was a crucial feature for their acceptance as valued members of staff, both by other members of staff, and by parents and the wider community.

It was hoped that, once the project was under way, staff who had shown less interest initially would consult with colleagues working with instructors, and become more aware of the potential benefits for the children. This did, in fact, happen. Before long, staff were requesting an instructor for particular lessons.

Gradually, the instructors gained confidence, and were very soon accepted by school staff as competent assistants. They were fully prepared to work with small groups of children, and aware that they need not deal only with children from one linguistic group. They each knew which children spoke the language with which they were primarily concerned, but if any other children wished to join in with an activity, they were encouraged to do so.

It was gratifying to walk into the nursery and find children who had been difficult, or timid, thoroughly engrossed in making chapattis, or joining in with stories, songs and action rhymes. And it was particularly heartening to find children from several linguistic groups, including monolingual English speakers, listening to stories told in Gujerati or Pushtu with complete attention, their eyes fixed upon the story-teller's face.

All instructors were concerned both with bilingual support in class-rooms, and with promoting a multicultural/multilingual ethos throughout the school. Parallel scripts were widely requested for label-ling, stories, and communications with parents. Activities such as dance, music, painting, needlework, history and geography were included in requests for assistance from teachers of older children, whilst a weekly session of cooking and sweet-making took place in the nursery. As lessons took place in the normal classroom setting, continuity was achieved between the activities of the language group and the rest of the class. Occasionally, an instructor was requested to work with the entire class with the assistance of the teacher, for example in teaching dances, or, on one occasion, in examining a variety of different spices, discussing their distinctive smells and labelling them in English and Punjabi.

In its early stages, the programme was very much exploratory, with instructors making perceptive and helpful comments concerning the level of children's language proficiency, and particular linguistic needs. One child who had been diagnosed as having a hearing problem was found to respond to his first language where he had ignored speakers of English.

Teachers involved with the project were pleasantly surprised to find that there were benefits for their children, without a lot of extra work for themselves. Evaluation was based upon comments from teachers, the responses of children and parents, and the progress made by some children. Several 5-year-olds had been struggling with mathematical concepts. An instructor sat with them and spoke to them in Urdu. It became obvious that the medium of instruction, and not the mathematical concepts, had been the problem.

In terms of acceptance and enthusiasm on the part of the children, the community and the school staff, the project was successful. In terms of impact, and educational achievement, the project's effect was limited, principally because of severe financial constraints. It had been envisaged that instructors' teaching commitments would gradually increase with the dictates of experience and demand. But, financially, this proved impossible. The demand was there, and we felt we had the experience to cope with it.

With hindsight, it was clear that the scope of the project and the extent of its potential should have been considered, from the outset, in relation to the constraints of funding and the availability of resources. The project was originally conceived as part of the school's community programme, and funds were meagre. In order to progress, as it undoubtedly has, the programme has needed to shift its ground. Bilingual support is now firmly established in the school, but, perceived as being a school-based programme, it is financed by the Local Education Authority as part of an initiative taking place in several schools, each operating to a similar pattern.

Just as any bilingual support programme needs access to the community, so the community must have access to the school, if there is to be mutual understanding between the school and its neighbourhood. One significant aim of community bilingual support is to increase sociolinguistic understanding on the part of the teachers involved, and to improve and consolidate educational understanding on the part of parents. In each school, there will be differences, and this must be acknowledged.

The philosophy of community bilingual support requires that its implications should be fully embraced. The school is part of the community. Successful educational practice depends upon close liaison between school and community, otherwise there can be no real awareness of the context in which a need has arisen, and by implication, a poor understanding of the conditions under which that need may be met. It is important to get out into the community and talk to children and their families. But it is far more important that we should listen to what they say.

Bibliography

APU (Assessment of Performance Unit) (1986) *Speaking and Listening: Assessment at Age 11*, Windsor: NFER–Nelson

Appel, R. and Muysken, P. (1987) *Language Contact and Bilingualism*, London: Edward Arnold

Baker, C. (1988) *Key Issues in Bilingualism and Bilingual Education*, Clevedon: Multilingual Matters Ltd.

Baetens Beardsmore, H. (1986) *Bilingualism: Basic Principles*, Clevedon: Multilingual Matters Ltd.

Bourne, J. (1989) *Moving into the Mainstream: LEA Provision for Bilingual Pupils*,Windsor: NFER–Nelson

Bronowski, J. (1973) *The Ascent of Man*, London: BBC

Brumfit, C. J. and Johnson, K. (eds) (1979) *The Communicative Approach to Language Teaching*, Oxford: Oxford Univeristy Press

Chatwin, R. (1984) 'Language in the multiracial classroom', in *Multiracial Education Review*, Vol. 2, Birmingham

Clark, M. (1988) *Children under Five: Educational Research and Evidence*, London: Gordon & Breach

Cockcroft Report (1982) *Mathematics Counts*, London: HMSO/DES

Cook, V. (1991) *Second Language Learning and English Teaching*, London: Edward Arnold

Cox Report (1988) *English for Ages 5 to 11*, London: HMSO/DES

DES (Department of Education and Science) (1975) *A Language for Life* (Bullock Report), London: HMSO

—— (1979) *Mathematics 5 to 11*, London: HMSO

—— (1987) *National Curriculum Task Group on Assessment and Testing: A Report*, London: HMSO

—— (1990) *English in the National Curriculum*, London: HMSO

Dodson, C. (1981) 'A Reappraisal of bilingual development and education', in H. Baetens Beardsmore (ed.), *Elements of Bilingual Theory*, Brussels: Vrije Universiteit

Donaldson, M. (1987) *Children's Minds*, London: Fontana

Grugeon, E. and Woods, P. (1990) *Educating All: Multicultural Perspectives in the Primary School*, London: Routledge

Halliday, M. A. K. (1968) 'Language and experience', in *Educational Review (The Place of Language)*, Vol. 20, No. 2 (February) Birmingham University

Hester, H. (1990) *Patterns of Learning*, London: CLPE

Houlton, D. (1985) *All Our Languages*, London: Edward Arnold

Katzner, K. (1986) *The Languages of the World* London: Routledge

Krashen, S. D. (1981) *Second Language Acquisition and Second Language Learning*, Oxford: Pergamon

Klein, W. (1986) *Second Language Acquisition*, Cambridge: Cambridge University Press

Linguistic Minorities Project (1985) *The Other Languages of England*, London: Routledge & Kegan Paul

McDonough, S. H. (1981) *Psychology in Foreign Language Teaching*, London: Allen & Unwin

Mercer, N., Czerniewska, P., Graddol, D., Edwards, V., Mayor, B., Maybin, J. and Sheldon, S. (1985) *Every Child's Language*, Milton Keynes: Open University Press

Naiman, N., Fröhlich, A. and Stern, H. (1975) *The Good Language Learner*, Toronto: Ontario Institute

NCMTT (1985) *Community Languages: The Supply and Training of Teachers*, York: National Council for Mother Tongue Teaching

Rees, O. A. and Fitzpatrick, F. (1981) *Report of the Mother Tongue and English Teaching Project*, Bradford: Bradford University

Saunders, G. (1988) *Bilingual Children: From Birth to Teens*, Clevedon: Multilingual Matters Ltd.

Selinker, L. (1972) 'Interlanguage', in *International Review of Applied Linguistics*, Vol. 10, No. 3

Singh, R. (1988) *Asian and White Perceptions of the Teaching Profession*, Bradford: Bradford and Ilkley Community College

Skutnabb-Kangas, T. (1990) *Language, Literacy and Minorities*, Clevedon: Minority Rights Group

Swann Report (1985) *Education for All*, London: HMSO/DES

Tansley, P. (1986) *Community Languages in Primary Education*, Windsor: NFER

Taylor, J. M. and Hegarty, S. (1985) *The Best of Both Worlds: A Review of Research into the Education of Pupils of South Asia Origin*, Windsor: NFER–Nelson

Tizard, B. and Hughes, M. (1984) *Young Children Learning, Talking and Thinking, at Home and at School*, London: Fontana

Tough, J. (1985) *Talk Two: Children Using English as a Second Language*, London: Onyx Press.

Vygotsky, S. (1984) *Thought and Language*, Cambridge, Mass.: MIT Press

Wells, G. (1987) *The Meaning Makers*, London: Hodder & Stoughton

Index